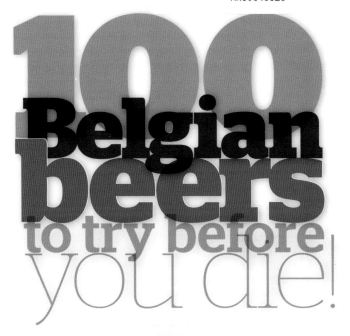

100 Belgian beers to try before you die!

Tim Webb & Joris Pattyn

BOOKS

For Emma –
belatedly. *TW*

Aan mijn vrouwtje Lut, die watertjes dronk en
BOB speelde, terwijl ik al de heerlijkheden proefde. *JPP*

Published by the Campaign for Real Ale Ltd.
230 Hatfield Road
St Albans
Hertfordshire AL1 4LW

www.camra.org.uk/books

© Campaign for Real Ale 2008

ISBN 978-1-85249-248-9

A CIP catalogue record for this book is
available from the British Library

Printed and bound in China by
1010 Printing International Ltd

Managing Editor: Simon Hall
Project Editors: Katie Hunt; Debbie Williams
Editorial Assistance: Emma Haines
Design/Typography: Dale Tomlinson
Typefaces: Village National and Stag
Cover design: Ian Midson
Photography: Katherine Longly
Map: John Plumer (JP Map Graphics Ltd)
Head of Marketing: Louise Ashworth

Acknowledgements and picture credits

The publisher would like to thank all the
breweries, distributers and others who have
kindly given permission for their photography
to be reproduced in this guide. Special thanks
go to Katherine Longly for her excellent,
commissioned photography at many breweries
and bars and to Chris 'Podge' Pollard for his help
with sourcing images.

Specific thanks go to: Belukus Marketing Inc.: 78;
CAMRA archive: 50 (above); CHARLES D COOK:
130 (left); CHRIS POLLARD: 51, 81 (below);
CHRIS POLLARD & SIBOHAN MCGINN: 126;
D&V International Inc.: 65, 106, 107, 108, 114 (left),
115 (below), 124, 125; KATHERINE LONGLY: back
cover 6–7, 12–13, 15, 16, 17, 18, 20, 22–23, 25, 26,
27 (left), 29 (above), 31, 32, 33, 39, 40–41, 47, 48
(left, below right), 49 (below), 50 (below), 54,
60–61, 62 (below), 63 (below), 66, 68, 69, 70–71,
72, 73, 75, 79 (above), 82–83, 84, 85 (above), 90
(below), 92, 95, 96, 98 (below), 99, 100, 101, 102,
104–105, 110, 112, 114 (right), 116–117, 118, 119, 120,
122, 123, 129, 134–135, 152–153; Shelton Brothers:
24 (right), 35, 36, 52, 89, 90 (above); TIM WEBB:
19, 51, 62 (above), 85 (below), 93, 94, 103, 111,
115 (above), 131 (above), 132 (right);
VANESSA COURTIER: 27 (right),
63 (above), 130 (right), 131 (below),
132 (left); Wetton Importers: 121

Contents

Introduction

JORIS AND I FIRST MET in a newly opened restaurant in Antwerp in 1992, while I was researching the first edition of the *Good Beer Guide Belgium*. In those days he was a mover and shaker – mainly shaker – in the Flemish beer consumer movement and I had recently given up the Chair of CAMRA's first publishing company, Alma Books.

From a wide-ranging menu I recall he chose a strange-sounding pie, containing both fish and meat, mainly on the grounds this was an unusual combination, even in that city of a thousand cuisines. I stuck with something more mainstream as I believe you should test new chefs on the way they cook staples. Each dish was more delicious than we had expected and we concluded this was a place with a good future. It is still there fifteen years later.

We have been taking different routes to the same conclusions ever since, sharing many hundreds of beers on the way. We now know each other well enough to disagree, sometimes passionately, though never in a way that really matters in the round.

Thirty years of travelling the world in search of top rate beers, and top rate judges of them, has persuaded me of three things:

First, the people who say that there is no such thing as a good or bad beer but only variations in matters of personal taste are talking kindergarten gibberish (or else have a lot of bad beer to sell).

Second, the appreciation of fine beer has little to do with a person's origins, life experiences, circumstances, or even exposure to beer over the years. Taste appreciation has a bit to do with age. Palates, like the people who own them, grow up a lot in their twenties. It has a lot to do with a person's mind – most particularly in how able the mind is to ignore soothing psychology of advertising and its virtual associations.

Finally, I have learned that recognising great craftsmanship in a beer and actually liking it are not the same thing. This, I feel sure, explains for the most part the occasional differences between Joris and myself in the text that follows. And the differences that each of us expects, confidently, that you will have with both of us.

More power to your discrimination, fellow traveller.

TIM WEBB
Cambridge, UK
Autumn 2007

Why Belgium?

BECAUSE OF THE ENDLESS variety of the styles of beer made there.

The theory goes that this diversity owes its origins to the habit of successive European overlords to wage war in its lands, regularly and brutally. People who live in a place that has been invaded and occupied more than thirty times in a thousand years tend to cling all the more strongly to their tried and tested local traditions and to harbour a fundamental mistrust of both big government and alien fashions.

As a result, the ways in which people make beer in the villages around, say, Kortrijk, Mechelen, Tournai and Aalst, may be equally excellent but remain true to local traditions, thereby ending up with virtually nothing in common except their raw ingredients.

When the late Michael Jackson first wrote about Belgian beers in the 1970s, he was marching into unclaimed territory. He pointed out to the world, indeed to Belgium itself, that these beers were an unsung cultural marvel, consciously avoiding use of the word 'disappearing'.

Thirty years on, it is still possible, thankfully, to find as wide an array of beers brewed in Belgium as one will find across most of the rest of the world. Some remain authentic to an age-old tradition of beer making found nowhere else on Earth, while others are modern inventions. Some are solid examples of top quality craftsmanship, while others are faintly crazed.

The last three decades have seen a struggle for survival by ancient brewing traditions and renewed pride in the best of these. This has occurred against a background of a world market obsessed with the creation of low cost, easy-drinking 'fast beers' with familiar names.

It seems likely that that struggle is now won, as craft beers have become a feature not only of the traditional brewing nations of Europe but also across North America, Australasia, southern Africa, South America and the Far East.

In the next decade the challenge will be to establish local and imported craft beers as a standard offering in quality hotels, restaurants and bars across the globe, where they belong. If quality beers can achieve that standing, their long-term future will be assured.

Prost!

Drinking at the Port Noire cellar-bar in Brussels

Glossary of beer styles

Abbey beers

Beers made in similar styles to some Trappist beers, such as *dubbel* and *tripel*, but which have no connection with a Trappist abbey. Some abbey beers have licensing arrangements with other religious orders. They range in quality from nectar to naff.

Ale

A beer fermented at room temperature, such that its yeast rises to the top – hence also 'top-fermented'.

Barley wine

A strong, usually sweet beer made from the best of grains. Designed for sipping rather than quaffing.

Dubbel

(Fr: *double*) Originally a beer that is fermented twice, designated XX from ancient times until the 19th century. Usually dark and on the sweetish side, though some are well attenuated.

Faro

A beer produced by reactivating pure *lambic* by the addition of a little sugar. Traditionally a draught beer found mainly in Brussels and Payottenland, it is sometimes found in bottled form. The term '*faro*' is protected by an EU Traditional Speciality Guaranteed (TSG) designation, which means that all products should be genuine.

Fruit lambic

A beer produced by steeping fruit in casks of *lambic*. Traditionally cherries (see oude kriek, below) or raspberries are used, but more recently brewers have experimented with using other types of fruit, such as strawberries, grapes and apricots.

Gueuze

Always '*gueuze*' in French, it appears in that spelling and also as '*geuze*' in Dutch. Under Belgian law a *gueuze* is a blended beer that must contain at least a dab of *lambic*, though a high proportion of other types of beers is allowed in the mix and this is what is found in most modern versions. For the real thing see *oude gueuze*.

Kriek

An old dialectic word for cherry, used for centuries to designate a beer that uses cherries in its production. The Belgian law that, in effect, allowed brewers to shove all sorts of non-lambic beer into *gueuze* also licensed them to put all manner of cherry-related gunk in *kriek*. Funnily enough, the Prime Minister of the day went on to become a non-Executive director of a global brewery whose products were let off the hook by this piece of consumer de-protection, a consideration possibly from the company's chairman, who was an agriculture minister at the time. For the authentic lambic version, see *oude kriek* (below). Non lambic-based cherry beers are known as *kreikenbier*.

Lager

An imprecise word that in the UK has come to refer to a dull blond style of easy-to-make beer for simple palates. Derived from the term 'lagering', or storage, an allusion to a time when mid-European brewers would put their lighter, bottom-fermented beers in cold storage for a couple of months before barrelling or bottling. The best still do.

Lambic

Collective term for all beers made by spontaneous fermentation and also the term used to mean the draught version of those beers taken straight from the cask. The principle of spontaneous fermentation is that the yeast that ferments the beer comes naturally from the atmosphere rather than being deliberately added. In practice, most brewers encourage the right kind of yeast to hang around at fermentation time, to make the process a little less random than it might be. Much like politics, really. A cask *lambic* that is six to twelve months old is referred to as young (Du: *jonge*), whilst those of two years ageing and above are termed old (Du: *oude*). Between the two it is a matter of judgement.

Oak-aged ales
(Du: *foeders*; Fr: *foudres*) Beers fermented in oak casks or tuns. These are usually, though not invariably, dark in colour and later blended and slightly sweetened. These were once the standard cask beer styles of large parts of Flanders.

Oud bruin
See 'oak-aged ales' (above). Some beers are actually aged in steel tanks with wood chips thrown into the fermenting beer to imitate the oak-ageing effects. This works with degrees of success that vary from quite a lot to none.

Oude gueuze
An authentic *gueuze* is a bottled beer, often with a Champagne-style liveliness, produced by blending young lambic with old and then reactivating it by the addition of a drop of liquid sugar. Traditional wines and ciders are spontaneously fermented by yeast caught in skins of the fruit and the overlap in tastes is often noticeable. The designation is protected by a TSG (see *faro*, above). The Flemish regional produce (Du: *streekproduct*) designation applies only to *oude gueuze* beers made in the Payottenland region, to the west and south of Brussels.

Oude kriek
Traditionally *kriek* was made by steeping cherries in an oak cask of *lambic* beer for around six months. It is still found on draught in a few cafés in Payottenland and Brussels but is mainly a bottled beer. The authentic version is protected by a TSG (see *faro*, above). To compare modern cherry beers with *oude kriek* is to put an alcopop alongside fine Beaujolais.

Saison
A style of beer associated mainly with the province of Hainaut and related to French *bière de garde* (or 'stored beer'). Traditionally made in the spring for consumption in the summer, when temperatures were too high for safe fermentation and the farm's brewery workers were needed in the fields. Highly hopped for better preservation in the short-term, it is likely that there were both light and strong versions. The association with farming has led to these being marketed as 'Farmhouse Ales' in the US and elsewhere.

Stout
A dark, bitter beer made with a relatively high proportion of chocolate malt and roasted barley. In West Flanders stout usually means a lowish strength (4 to 5% abv), intensely sweet ale.

Trappist beer
Any beer sanctioned by one of the seven official brewing abbeys of the Trappist order. No other beer may call itself Trappist.

Tripel
(Fr: *triple*.) Originally a beer that is fermented three times, designated XXX in ancient times. Always a strong beer and historically dark. Since the 1930s the term has come to mean a strong blonde ale, as pioneered by the Trappist brewery at Westmalle.

Wheat beer
(Du: *tarwebier*; Fr: *bière de froment*.) See 'white beer' below.

White beer
(Du: *witbier*; Fr: *bière blanche*.) A beer that is usually but not always blonde, hazy, low in alcohol (4 to 5% abv) and, in Belgium, flavoured. Its key feature is that the mash contains roughly 30% wheat, the haze comes from a suspension of fine wheat flour. Traditionally dried citrus peel, coriander and other spices are added at the brewing stage.

Winter beer
Typically a dark, strong and highly-spiced beer.

Glossary of tasting terms

Brettanomyces
A genus of slow-fermenting yeast that is essential to the development of vintage character in wines and in oak-aged beers. *Brettanomyces lambicus* adds the 'horse blanket' aroma and characteristic rustic flavours to older lambic beers.

Brouwmeester
(Fr: *maître brasseur*; Ge: *Bräumeister*) Originally a qualified and articled brewer (cf. Master Brewer). Nowadays the term used for the head brewer. Used affectionately to describe the owners of one-man operation microbreweries.

Candy sugar
Said to be an odourless and flavourless type of sugar. Used by brewers to add alcoholic strength without adding additional grain flavours. In practice stronger beers can absorb some without harming their character, though it does have slight odours and flavours and when used to excess creates a lightweight beer in a heavyweight form.

Carbon dioxide
Also CO_2. The gas produced by the fermentation of sugar into alcohol, which if added artificially to beer will send some British beer drinkers into a state of apoplexy.

Esters
Complex organic chemical found in tiny amounts in beers and many other foodstuffs, often adding highly specific flavours and aromas. Many hundreds have been isolated in beer. (Esteric = of esters.)

Fusels
Alcohols of higher molecular weight.

Head
(Fr: *mousse*; US: *suds*) An aesthetic necessity in the dominant beer drinking classes of our day but not an essential ingredient. There is a book to be written about the political, economic and social significance of the froth on top of a beer.

Hops
Technically these are flowers of the hop bine. Almost all of the world's hop production goes to beer making. Used as flavourings and preservatives in beer for over a thousand years, they have been a standard ingredient of beer since the 12th or 13th centuries. All were originally varietals or cross-breeds though some have remained the same for a century or more. They vary in bitterness, aroma, taste and preservative qualities, as well as yield and susceptibility to disease.

Lace
The remnants left by the head as it retreats down the glass.

Malt
Barley grain that has been allowed to germinate at the maltings before being roasted to varying degrees to capture its sugars and maximum tastiness and in varying degrees of caramelisation.

Mouthfeel
The impression that the beer gives in the mouth.

Nose
Posh word for the smell of the beer. Preferred to aroma as this can also refer to a single smell within a complex of smells.

Oxidation
Alcohol and other flavours in beer can oxidise when they come into contact with air, causing the formation of aldehydes and acids. Even in small amounts this can add pleasant, challenging or unpleasant tastes.

Retronasal
Tastes and aromas that are appreciated after swallowing and feel as though they come from the back of one's nose or palate.

Residual sugar
Unfermented sugar that is sometimes there

because the beer is still developing. More usually deliberate and caused by the presence of sugar types that ordinary yeast cannot ferment.

Slick (mouthfeel)
Liquid but not watery.

Spritzy
Gaseous and lively but not fizzy as such.

Tannins
A group of chemicals found in some foodstuffs, notably tea and red wine, that give a woody flavour characteristic. Many tannin effects in oak-aged beers are not from the wood at all but just taste that way.

Texture
The substance of the beer.

UFOs
Unidentified Floating Objects.

Underbuild
A set of complex of flavours and textures that contribute the main building blocks to a (usually complicated) beer.

Underlay
The flavour and texture of the grain base in a beer.

Yeast
Collective term for the strain of micro-organisms used to ferment beer and some other alcoholic beverages.

Yeasty
A flavour characteristic suggesting that the rougher products of fermentation are still obvious.

The Beers

North Sea

NETHERLANDS

Zeebrugge

Ostend

Bruges (Brugge)

Veurne

Antwerp

Sint Niklaas

Turnhout

Herentals

Lier

Ghent

Dendermonde

Mechelen (Malines)

Roeselare

Deinze

Aalst

Leuven

Hasselt

Ieper (Ypres)

Kortrijk (Courtrai)

Oudenaarde (Audenarde)

Geraardsbegen

Ninove

Brussels (Bruxelles)

Halle

Sint Truiden

Tongeren

Enghien

Tubize

Leuze

Tournai

Ath (Aat)

Soignies

Genappe

Liège (Luik)

Verviers

Mons (Bergen)

Charleroi

Namur

Huy

Thuin

Dinant

Marche en Famenne

Chimay

Bastogne

FRANCE

Arlon

N

50 km
50 miles

FEATURED BREWERIES

1	Abbaye des Rocs	20	Dubuisson	38	Rochefort
2	Achel	21	Dupont	39	Rodenbach
3	Achouffe	22	Duvel Moortgat	40	Rulles
4	Anker	23	Fantôme	41	Saint Feuillien
5	Bavik	24	Girardin	42	Sint-Bernardus
6	Blaugies	25	Glazen Toren	43	Sint Canarus
7	Boon	26	Hanssens	44	Slaghmuylder
8	Brabant	27	't Hofbrouwerijke	45	Strubbe
9	Brootcoorens	28	Kerkom	46	Struise Brouwers
10	de Cam	29	Loterbol	47	Val-Dieu
11	Cantillon	30	Malheur	48	Van Den Bossche
12	Caracole	31	Martens	49	Van Eecke
13	Chimay	32	Mort Subite	50	Van Honsebrouck
14	Cnudde	33	Orval	51	Vapeur
15	Contreras	34	Proef	52	Verhaeghe
16	De Koninck	35	Vicaris	53	Walrave
17	De Ryck	36	de Ranke	54	Westmalle
18	de Dolle Brouwers	37	Regenboog	55	Westvleteren
19	Drie Fonteinen				

Abbaye des Rocs (US: Brasserie des Rocs)

Blanche des Honnelles (US: Blanche Double)

6% alcohol by volume

beer style Wheat beer

33 cl & **75** cl bottles and on draught

Importer Beer Direct

Importer D&V International

THE ABBAYE DES ROCS brewery began life in 1979, in a pretty village set among the hills by the French border, southwest of Mons. It was one of the first new breweries in Belgium for forty years. Not that many people noticed – in those days it produced the equivalent of four crates of beer a week.

Thirty years on, this is a thriving microbrewery producing high quality ales that are good enough to be exported across Europe and North America.

Blanche des Honnelles began life in 1991 as a local beer, taking its name from a stream that runs near the brewery. The brewery's stronger ales are spiced rather obviously. In contrast, this beer, made in the Belgian style that is most frequently associated with spicing, is remarkably restrained.

Brasserie de l'Abbaye des Rocs
37 Chaussée Brunehault, 7387 Montignies-sur-Roc
T 065 75 59 99   **F** 065 75 59 98
E abbaye.des.rocs@skynet.be
www.abbaye-des-rocs.com

Group visits only, by arrangement.
If you are into drinking beers as close as possible to where they are produced then the **Château** café (7 Place Fulgence Masson, Montignies-sur-Roc) is your best bet. A barn of a place, overlooking the village green, it opens every day except Tuesday, from 11.00.

TASTING NOTES

This is a pale gold-yellow beer with a greenish sheen and a compact, collapsing white head. The nose is citrus, like mandarins with a sweet under-lay – *Mandarine Napoléon* liqueur maybe. There is subdued coriander, a bit of orange peel, a slight peppery aroma. The taste begins dry and slightly orangey, herbal and peppery, yet the base is sweet. At the back of the nose, on swallowing, one gets bitterish flavours. The mouthfeel is dry, with some warming from alcohol, which dents its ability to refresh. Is that spicy-herbal aftertaste rhubarb?

VERDICT

Along with **St. Bernardus Witbier** (p. 108), this is currently the best Belgian wheat beer in our view. While admiring the effectiveness of Pierre Celis and others in reviving the Belgian style of 'white' beer, neither of us is a huge fan of the sweet and heavily spiced variety. Blanche des Honnelles is sizeably different.

15

Achelse Kluis Trappist 5° Blond

5% alcohol by volume

Beer style Blonde ale

On draught only

UK importer This beer is never exported. It is found only at the brewery tap

US importer This beer is never exported. It is found only at the brewery tap

ABBEYS THAT ARE homes to a variety of monastic orders have for centuries brewed beer for consumption by the brothers, their lay workers and guests. The hospitality of their inns and guesthouses was one of the things that made them so popular with the well-travelled of mediaeval Europe.

The only monasteries that still oversee brewing operations are those of the Trappist Order. There are six official Trappist breweries in Belgium, plus one just over the Dutch border at Koningshoeven, near Tilburg. Their beers increasingly use the term Trappist in their name and bear the 'Authentic Trappist Product' logo.

Over the last three decades, Trappist beers have gained international recognition for their excellence, some with more justification than others. The creation of a new Trappist brewery in 1999 caused quite a stir, all the more for its intentions to supply draught beers of regular strength, rather than the stronger bottled beers that had become the norm at other abbey breweries.

TASTING NOTES

This dark golden beer with a greenish sheen offers a good white head that recedes slowly. The nose is a perfect balance of combined dry malts and good Saaz-like hops. The taste is no different, a nice, clean hop and dry pale malts taste. At the back of the nose are undeniably perfumed hops as well as an aroma of palm trees, with a slight almond flavour in the aftertaste. It is a light-bodied and refreshing beer.

VERDICT

Of the two lighter, draught beers, each found only at the cloisters, this is the one that most regularly impresses visiting beer lovers. Brewpub simplicity meets traditional Trappist quality to make an agreeable light ale that is worth pedalling or riding a fair distance to discover.

Brewery information See p. 17

♥ Achelse Kluis Trappist Extra Bruin

9.5% alcohol by volume

er style   Strong abbey-style ale

🍾   **75** cl bottles and occasionally **100** cl bottles

importer   Beer Direct

importer   Shelton Brothers

EVEN MONASTIC BREWERIES must have a business plan. They work to make money for the Order and its charitable works.

When Achel, on the Dutch border in an attractive, quiet corner of northern Limburg, started brewing in 1998, their plan was to produce ordinary-strength draught beers first and then move into stronger, bottled beers. A stronger blond came first, and then a stronger brown. Eventually, one Christmas came **Drie Wijzen** (Three Wise Men). This was the beer that spawned this year-round special, 'Extra', the personal favourite of the brouwmeester.

TASTING NOTES

Achel Extra is dark chestnut in colour, with an amber sheen. Its thick yellowish head collapses to leave lacy rings. With a nose of dark roasted malts, chocolate fondant, pecan nuts and a slight oxidation, it is impressively complex. The taste is quite sweet, chocolaty and nutty, with more hops retro-

nasally. The mouthfeel has a touch of walnut oil to it, with CO_2 stimulation adding to the texture.

VERDICT

All in all a nice rich beer, which some might think could do with a good dose of American hops. Well worth looking for, either as a Christmas treat or for regular cellar stock.

Brouwerij der Sint Benedictusabdij de Achelse Kluis
Kluis 1, 3930 Hamont-Achel
T 011 80 07 60   **E** brouwerij@achelsekluis.be
www.achelsekluis.org

The cloisters at Achel house a refectory from which the brewery installation can be seen. There is also a large outside terrace where you can park your bicycle or tie up your horse. It is open to the public every day except Monday (11.00–17.30 May–Sep, 12.00–17.00 other times).

There is also a beer shop (Tue–Sat 09.00–12.00 & 12.30–17.00) and a conference facility.

Houblon Chouffe

9% alcohol by volume

Beer style Bitter beer

33 cl & **75** cl bottles

UK importer This beer is not imported to the UK yet

US importer Duvel USA

THE BRASSERIE D'ACHOUFFE, in the hamlet of Achouffe, near the Luxembourg province market town of Houffalize, was a 'hobby that got out of hand' for Chris Bauweraerts and friends. So much so that when Duvel Moortgat bought them out in 2006, working became an option rather than an obligation.

FAQs

Q Is a *chouffe* an elf of local legend?

A *No, we made a gnome and called it a chouffe.*

Q Why a gnome on the label?

A *Because everyone else has a monk.*

Q Why brew with spring water?

A *Because there is no other water in the village.*

Q What is the significance of the violin-shaped glasses?

A *They are the cheapest.*

Originally, India Pale Ale (IPA) referred to strong, amber-coloured ales that were loaded with hops in order to preserve them on the long sea journey from England to the India of empire. Although retained for some low gravity bitters in the UK, internationally it is coming to signify a strong, bitter, amber ale once more.

TASTING NOTES

The huge whipped-egg-white head collapses into off-white rings, over a hazy yellowish beer with a greenish sheen. Hops invade the nose but in a way that is more European than American. Dried mandarins join the nose somehow as well. Hop bitterness dominates the flavour too, with orange zest and dry hopping, though no Cascade – this is not the US West Coast. Tannin and pine emphasise the hop character. It has an appropriately resinous, oily mouthfeel and texture, and is medium to well-bodied. It ends on a dry aftertaste.

VERDICT

A good beer, if a little unsubtle. Subtitled 'Dobbelen IPA Tripel', whatever that means, it was clearly made for the US market, to compete with that country's new breed of 'hop monster' beers. Nonetheless, it has something Belgian to say for itself. A modern hybrid for a global market.

Brasserie d'Achouffe
Rue du Village 32, 6666 Achouffe
T 061 28 81 47   **F** 061 28 82 64
E info@achouffe.be
www.achouffe.be

Group tours happen at 10.30 each day and if numbers are low you may be allowed to join on spec.

At the rear of the brewery building is the **Bistro**, which opens from 09.00 to 21.00 every day except Wednesday and daily in high summer. From its dining area you can see the goings-on in the brewhouse.

Gouden Carolus Classic

8.5% alcohol by volume

beer style Strong brown ale

🛢 **33** cl & **75** cl bottles and on draught

importer Beer Direct

importer Wetten Importers

MECHELEN, MIDWAY BETWEEN Antwerp and Brussels, has numerous claims to fame. It was the terminal for Europe's first ever commercial railway line; it has the tallest cathedral tower in Belgium; and for centuries it was a major centre for the production of brown ales.

Nowadays, its one remaining brewery has a reasonable claim to be Belgium's oldest, tracing its origins back to 1369 and possibly earlier. Its classically proportioned brown ale is named after a gold coin from the reign of Charles V (1500–1556).

There is a public brewing demonstration on 24th February each year, to celebrate the birthday of Hapsburg Emperor Charles V, who grew up in the town. They brew **Cuvée van de Keizer** on that day, an 11% abv beer based on the Classic.

There is also an open day on the first Saturday in July to accompany the Beer Brothers' beer festival (*see* www.thebeerbrothers.be).

Brewery information
See p. 20

TASTING NOTES

Gouden Carolus Classic is a dark red-brown beer under a slim, brownish head that leaves neat rings of lace. Its characteristic aroma features raisin and sultana in a fruity, alcoholic nose, reminiscent of a rich Christmas cake. The taste is outspokenly sweet, alcoholic and awash with fruity esters, suggesting fresh figs, plums, pears, dried dates and brandy. Imagine a soup made from fruit cake. The texture is a bit thin, strangely at odds with its rich flavour profile and significant strength.

VERDICT

The brewery has applied the Gouden Carolus brand name to many of its beers in recent years but this beer remains the classic in every sense.

BREWERY

Anker

🍷 Gouden Carolus Noël

10% alcohol by volume

Beer style   Winter beer

🍾 🛢   **33** cl, **75** cl & **150** cl bottles and on draught

UK importer   Beer Direct

US importer   Wetten Importers

THE ANCHOR BREWERY may have the oldest pedigree in Belgium, but its greatest developments have been in the last ten years. Having been in the same family for five generations, it had been struggling until Charles Leclef took charge in 1998.

Since taking the helm, Leclef has comprehensively overhauled the old range of beers, invested heavily in the brewery and its site, galvanised export and created several new beers. Of these, **Gouden Carolus Easter** and **Gouden Carolus Tripel** are good but this one is our favourite.

TASTING NOTES

Imagine staring into a dark, deep-red sea that has rubies sparkling within it. If the appearance does not make you dizzy, the nose of fortified Madeira wine, raisins, roasted malts and molasses should. Diving into the taste, you find immediately a spritzy acidity, followed by fruity esters. The, typically Gouden Carolus, aftertaste also has a fruity character with fruit acids bound up in it. Equally typical, the body is thinner than expected, but with the unmistakable throat-warming effect of alcohol.

VERDICT

Typical of the dark, strong, spicy type of Christmas beer that has grown in popularity once more in recent years. To sample the complete range of Belgium's Christmas beers visit the Essen winter beer festival (*see* **www.kerstbierfestival.be**).

Brouwerij Het Anker
Guido Gezellelaan 49, 2800 Mechelen
T 015 28 71 47   **F** 015 28 71 48
E het.anker@pandora.be
www.hetanker.be

The brewery's massive on-site café, the **Anker** is open every day except Wednesday, from 11.30, and serves an adventurous menu (12.00–15.00; 18.00–22.30) plus all the brewery's beers on draught. There is a beer shop too, stocking some rarer brews. This is currently the only Belgian brewery to run a hotel on site. The 22-room **Hotel Carolus** (**T** 015 28 71 41; **F** 015 28 71 42; **E** hotel@hetanker.be) is comfortable but not plush and can be booked through the brewery website.

Petrus Aged Pale

7.3% alcohol by volume

beer style   Aged pale ale

33 cl bottles only

importer Beer Direct

importer Global Beer Network

THE BAVIK BREWERY is run by the fourth generation of the De Brabandere family to own it since it
was founded in 1894. Recent years have seen a
significant expansion of the company, with investment in a new brewhouse, a couple of pub chains
and various new brands.

A small part of this investment involved going
back to the future. Some years ago, Bavik were
persuaded by their US importers to bottle some of
their oak-aged pale ale in its neat state. Until that
time it had been used exclusively as a mixer beer in
the blending of some sweet-and-sour brown ales.

After even more pressure from Belgian beer
lovers, they have recently decided to release some
of this 'export' beer to the local market too.

NV Bavik SA
Rijksweg 33, 8531 Bavikhove   **T** 056 71 90 91
F 056 71 15 12   **E** info@bavik.be   **www.bavik.be**

Group visits only, by arrangement.

TASTING NOTES

Petrus Aged Pale has a dark golden-yellow,
dusty-hazy colour. Acidity is usually detrimental
to head stability but despite this it sports a stable
white head. The nose is vinous and woody, with
discernible lactic and acetic acid turning fruity,
with lemon and green apple. The flavour speaks
of careful ageing, wood being discernible among
mellow acidity that includes a little acetic. The
beer is built on a firm malt presence, hints of
sweetness coming from unfermentable sugars.
There is an unmistakable acid-burn in the
mouthfeel and on swallowing, while in the
aftertaste there are long woody notes.

VERDICT

This beer is the epitome of an oak-aged ale with
the exception of its pale colour. Definitely one to
seek out for its unusual but authentic character.

Rodenbach's oak tuns (see p. 96)

Bière Darbyste

5.8% alcohol by volume

Beer style Regional specialty

37.5 cl & 75 cl bottles

UK importer Belgian Beer Import (Bierlijn)

US importer Shelton Brothers

THE VILLAGE OF BLAUGIES is just south of Dour, to the southwest of Mons. Pierre-Alex Carlier and Marie-Robert Pourtois set up their splendid craft brewery beyond its southern edge, three hundred metres from the French border, in 1988.

The styles of beer brewed reflect what Pierre-Alex calls, "the beers I like to drink". No boring old market analysis here.

This particular beer reminds him of one made by his grandmother, with figs in the mash as a nod to Pastor Darby, a local preacher who enabled his congregation to defy a local ban on alcohol by declaring that the brown liquid they were caught drinking was a concoction of fig juice.

TASTING NOTES

Darbyste is usually a hazy, golden-orange beer, with little flecks that present themselves conspicuously on an otherwise virgin-white, full head. There is a certain vegetable sweetness and slight sourness in the nose, presumably due to the 'fig juice'. The taste says that there is something going on in there – dry to the point of faint sourness, slight spicing too and a little fruit. There is no sweetness in the taste unless you try it at the brewery, when there remains some sugar and fig character. Even then it ends with a dry, sharp-sour finish.

VERDICT

A light blonde ale in an unusual style. Nice – but this is one of the few beers JPP prefers to drink young.

Brewery information See p. 26

La Moneuse

8% alcohol by volume

beer style Strong amber ale

37.5 cl & **75** cl bottles

importer Belgian Beer Import (Bierlijn)

importer Shelton Brothers

IN KEEPING WITH the theme of doing things incorrectly, La Moneuse is beer named after a local brigand called Antoine-Joseph Moneuse (1768–1797), who followed up an unfortunate childhood by robbing people he thought were rich, on the grounds that they may be responsible for some of the world's ills. His forte was stripping them naked and then burning their feet in an effort to get them to say where their stash was hidden.

Marie-Robert Pourtois is convinced she is his descendant. Anyone accidentally leaving the Fourquet café-restaurant and its impressive open griddle without paying, please note.

TASTING NOTES

La Moneuse gushes into a thick head, interspersed with big bubbles. The beer itself is orange-amber and usually hazy. The nose is at first spicy with coriander, before becoming chalky and a little rusty, finishing on yeast, citrus and candy sugar. The taste is spicy too, with more coriander, white pepper and a little something else. There is some sweetness but more tartness. The palate is yeasty, earthy and again rusty, with a background bitterness that is more like the inner peel of walnuts, than of hops. The impression is of quite a dry, medium to well-bodied beer.

VERDICT

A down-to-earth, spiced amber beer that is all the more likeable for being one of a kind.

Brewery information *See p. 26*

BREWERY Blaugies

Saison d'Epeautre

6% alcohol by volume
Beer style Wheat beer
37.5 cl & **75** cl bottles only
UK importer Belgian Beer Import (Bierlijn)
US importer Shelton Brothers

A YEAR OR TWO BACK the process of handing Blaugies brewery on to the next generation began. Son Cédric has taken over the running of the café-restaurant. His brother Kevin has become the brewer, though how much freedom he gets to experiment with the heirlooms is questionable. At present he is happy that his customers can detect no change in the beers.

This example is based on an ancient variant of wheat called *spelt*, sourced from Germany.

TASTING NOTES

Do not be taken aback if Saison d'Epeautre gushes a bit after being uncorked, or if the heavy protein haze from the *spelt* fails to unclump itself. It should still form a huge yellowish head that collapses above a peach-gold, hazy beer. The aroma is tricky. Something doggy at first, then lemon or grapefruit peel, some honeyed-flowery wafts, and something herbal and nectar-laden, like spring flowers. Some bitterness from hops – unusual in a wheat beer – and a tart taste, with spices, herbs and grasses appearing, and a little zest from an unidentifiable citrus fruit. There is a slight tang of metal oxide too. Light but not empty, it manages to end dry.

VERDICT

This is the Blaugies classic. A unique beer that manages to be true to the original saison style while also being a variant on wheat beer. Extremely refreshing and a great summer drink. If the world of beer ever decides to go crazy about well-hopped beers brewed from *spelt* this is bound to remain a front-runner.

Brasserie de Blaugies
Rue de la Frontière 435, 7370 Dour (Blaugies)
T&F 065 65 03 60
E info@brasseriedeblaugies.com
www.brasseriedeblaugies.com

The brewery has a simple but excellent café-restaurant on site, housed in a modern barn conversion. Called the **Fourquet**, it opens Wednesday to Sunday from 11.00 to 23.00. Its restaurant (12.00–14.00 & 18.00–21.30) features top quality locally-sourced meat cooked on an open grill in the middle of the dining area.

There is a meeting room with some teaching aids, for up to 30 people. A long-promised 9-bedroom hotel has not yet materialised.

On Whitsun weekend the whole village, including the brewery, opens its doors to the public.

Boon

Oude Geuze Boon Mariage Parfait

8% alcohol by volume

er style Oude gueuze

37.5 cl bottles only (**75** cl bottles US only)

mporter Cave Direct

mporter Vanberg & DeWulf

FRANK BOON took over the De Vits lambic brewery at Lembeek, near Halle, south of Brussels in 1977. This was at a time when the resuscitation trolley had been withdrawn from the ward where traditional lambic beers were living out their final days.

All the brewing pundits of the time thought he was mad but persistence and pragmatism have seen him through.

The bulk of his production is of lambic beers that are commercially orientated. However, he still makes two authentic oude gueuze beers, of which the Mariage Parfait (or "perfect marriage") is the top of the range.

TASTING NOTES

This gueuze sports a pale ochre colour. Its slight white head is quite stable. The nose reeks of 'horse blanket' (the thumbprint of lambic's Brettanomyces yeast), with lemon and lactic acid. In the mouth we again encounter lemon and Brettanomyces, with the typical flavour of an apple pie made with bruised apples, a little sulphur and the distinctly cheesy flavour of aged hops. The mouthfeel is very refreshingly spritzy without being fizzy. There is an aftertaste of saddle soap and old hop cones.

VERDICT

An authentic olde-style gueuze that feels well-constructed rather than the product of a riot.

Brewery information *See p. 28*

Boon

Oude Kriek Boon

6.5% alcohol by volume
Beer style Oude kriek
37.5 cl & **75** cl bottles
UK importer Cave Direct
US importer Vanberg & DeWulf

AFTER SEVERAL YEARS of fighting an uphill battle for recognition and a legitimate market, Frank Boon finally made a deal with the Palm brewery that in effect keeps the business going by providing a large outlet for simpler cherry beers and a sweeter form of gueuze, while the serious business of making some smaller-scale authentic beers goes on behind the scenes.

His cherry beers, both the commercial and the more authentic, have the highest fruit content of any of the lambic brewers. His draught *krieken-lambic*, which all his cherry beers contain, can occasionally be found served straight from the barrel and is commendably dry.

TASTING NOTES

Oude Kriek Boon is beer at its most beautiful – a superb garnet red liquid under a pink rosé head, which is remarkably stable for its acidity. The nose is a classic example of the marriage of cherries, 'horse blanket', wet wood, a vague smokiness and a jumble of organic acids. The taste is at once extremely tart and tannin-rich, against a backdrop of full-on fruit – sour cherry, green apple and redcurrant. The mouthfeel gives the expected drying effect, as if attacking the tartar of ones' teeth. There is perhaps too much body – a sign of young lambic in the blend – yet the finish is still very acidic, albeit with lots of red fruit.

VERDICT

Surprisingly controlled for an old-style kriek, its drinkability is more restrained than some. This is still not one for the faint hearted.

Boon NV
Fonteinstraat 65, 1502 Lembeek
T 02 356 66 44   **F** 02 356 33 99   **E** info@boon.be
www.boon.be

Group visits only, by arrangement.
Tours usually end up at the **Kring** café in Lembeek (15 Stevens Dewaelplein), next to the church in the village centre, which opens every day except Monday, from 10.00. All of the brewery's beers are usually available, plus some basic bar snacks.

La Brabançonne Blonde au Miel

6.5% alcohol by volume

er style   Blonde ale

   75 cl bottles only

mporter   The beers of the Brabant brewery are not exported yet

mporter   The beers of the Brabant brewery are not exported yet

THE VILLAGE OF Baisy-Thy is just off the N5 between Brussels and Charleroi, in Brabant-Wallon, the Belgian province with the least well-developed beer culture of modern times.

The Brasserie du Brabant opened in October 2002 in an old farmhouse, using makeshift kit. We may have been optimistic including one of their beers here. They are inconsistent, like many tiny breweries, but they do hit the heights with great regularity.

The label on this beer reads: "Made from pale malt and artisanally produced honey. Without becoming too sweet, it remains refreshing, and ideal for an afternoon in the sun." If all commercial descriptions were so accurate, tasting notes would become obsolete.

TASTING NOTES

This beer is pale yellow like pineapple juice, crowned by a huge, stable, creamy, light yellow head that leaves some lacing. Its hazy appearance is fine yeast in suspension, at a guess. The nose is idiosyncratic of a Wallonian farmhouse brewery, yielding spring flowers, honey, spice and some citrus. The taste is surprisingly bitter, in a flowery-spicy sort of way, and even a tad harsh. The honey leaves some flavour but no sweetness, while the finish betrays a slight acidity. Although well-attenuated the malts and honey leave an imprint. Light in character, the beer is not at all light in body.

VERDICT

A surprising and interesting brew. Seldom will you find such a well-attenuated honey beer. A better choice of hops could make it breathtaking.

La Brasserie du Brabant
59 Rue Banterlez, 1470 Baisy-Thy
T 067 79 18 79
E labrasseriedubrabant@skynet.be
www.labrasseriedubrabant.tk

Phone ahead and they will show you round, provided they are in and it is clear that you want to buy some beer.

Angelus Blonde

7% alcohol by volume

Beer style Blonde ale

75 cl and occasionally **150** cl bottles

UK importer The beers of the Brootcoorens brewery are not exported yet

US importer The beers of the Brootcoorens brewery are not exported yet

ALAIN BROOTCOORENS is a local hero. After a decade of dreaming about it, he created his own brewery in 2000, in the small border town of Erquelinnes, southwest of Mons, the first and last stop for slow trains from and to France.

Our impression is that he gets great pleasure from his craft but is not in brewing to make a fortune. So whether his rather pleasant beers will ever reach foreign parts – or even the city of Mons – with any regularity, is questionable.

TASTING NOTES

Angelus Blonde presents a generous, fine, light-yellowish head over a golden beer with an orange sheen. There is a heavy deposit in the bottle. A perfumed, grassy nose has fresh and dried wild herbs, spring flowers, pale malt and just a pinch of caramalt. The initial taste is of bitter herbs, though in the absence of roasted malts this diminishes rapidly. The character is of a pale malts beer that is dry with no discernible residual sugars, though there follows a hay-like flavour with a whiff of horseradish or mustard seed. Light to medium-bodied, with mouthfeel to match. This is no empty beer, a refreshing character relieving unhoppy bitterness.

VERDICT

This is a typically untypical Wallonian blonde ale, not made to imitate its peers but rather to be interestingly different from them.

Brasserie Brootcoorens
Rue de Mauberge 197, 6560 Erquelinnes
T&F 071 55 86 66
E angelus.br@swing.be
www.brasserie-brootcoorens-erquelinnes.be

The brewery is open for direct sales every Saturday (09.00–12.00; 13.30–17.00).

During the week, the most reliable outlet in town is the **Commerce** café opposite the railway station (338 Rue Roi Albert 1er), which opens every day except Sunday, from 10.30 to 20.30.

de Cam

🍷 de Cam Oude Geuze

6.5% alcohol by volume

beer style Oude gueuze

🍾 **37.5** cl & **75** cl bottles

importer Belgian Beer Import (Bierlijn)

importer The beers from De Cam are not exported to the US yet

LAMBIC BEERS come in three varieties. First there are the draught lambic beers, brewed as any other prior to their odd fermentation. Then there are the gueuze beers, made by blending the beers from young and old draught lambics and then bottling them. Then there are the kriek and other fruit beers, made by steeping fruit in casks of lambic.

All but three producers nowadays brew their own lambics and rely on these to be the building blocks from which all their beers are made. However, this is a modern trend. In years gone by, most producers bought in their lambics from elsewhere to blend or steep them to whatever was their local preference.

When it opened in 1997, at Gooik, in the Payottenland west of Brussels, de Cam became the first new *geuzestererij* or blender for forty years. Its first *steker* in chief was Willem van Herreweghen, one of the most highly regarded brewers of his generation, whose day job was as brewing director of the Palm brewery group.

More recently Karel Goddeau, head brewer at Slaghmuylder and one of the best of the next generation, has taken over.

TASTING NOTES
De Cam Oude Geuze's pale hazy orange colour makes it look a bit like a wheat beer, though its huge, fluffy white head dissipates swiftly. The jumble of aromas – yoghurt, 'horse blanket', lemon, wet wood, grapefruit and pineapple set the scene. It may be new-fangled but this is an authentic old-style gueuze. It is completely unsweetened and thus marvellously refreshing. Vintages vary but it is always tart, even when not outspoken. Pineapple, wood and lactic acid are among its flavours. Until recently it featured little acid burn, though the aftertaste featured a long, soft lactic tail. Recent efforts have been more daring.

VERDICT
Surprisingly good, right from the start. Now comfortably sitting among the best of the traditional gueuzes.

Enjoying a glass of de Cam Oude Geuze at Kaffee de Hopduvel, Ghent

Brewery information *See p. 32*

🍷 de Cam Oude Kriek

6.5% alcohol by volume

Beer style Oude kriek

🍾 **37.5** cl & **75** cl bottles

UK importer Belgian Beer Import (Bierlijn)

US importer The beers from De Cam are not exported to the US yet

FROM THE START de Cam was dedicated to traditional production methods, without cutting corners. So when they realised that the delightful old oak casks bought at a sharp price from the Pilsener Urquell brewery in the Czech Republic

were in fact lined with exactly the same sealant as most metal barrels, it had to come off – making them not quite the bargain they had been.

So it was with making their Oude Kriek. 'Kriek' means 'cherry' in various old dialects. These have been steeped in lambic for centuries, as one of the means of using up a crop with a short season and predictable annual glut.

The cherries impart colour, sweetness and flavour, the last of these relying in part on the stones remaining in the fruit. So when de Cam uses cherries, the stones remain in the fruit.

TASTING NOTES

Because De Cam Oude Kriek is made in the old-fashioned way, it pours with virtually no head on the clear, red beer. The vinous nose, fruity but not expressly cherried, is alluring. There is a lot of fresh sour cherry in the taste, without any dominant lambic, though it is clearly acidic. The fuller background flavour is down to the cherry stones. Surprisingly it comes pretty carbonated – almost too much.

VERDICT

Not a bad start at all. There is every indication that we will be able to wax lyrical over future incarnations.

Geuzestekerij De Cam
Dorpsstraat 67A, 1755 Gooik
T 02 532 21 32
www.decam.be

The lambics from which de Cam's beers are made are matured in large oak casks salvaged from the Pilsner Urquell brewery in the Czech Republic. These are housed in a country crafts museum in the centre of Gooik. The brewer is often around on Sunday afternoons to tell a fuller story.

The centre's café, the **Cam** is open daily from 11.00 and serves the base draught lambic and *kriekenlambic* via handpump into traditional drinking crocks. They also serve food (11.30–14.00 & 17.30–20.30), and other beers.

Cantillon

Brasserie Cantillon SPRL
Rue Gheude 56, 1070 Bruxelles (Anderlecht)
T 02 521 49 28   F 02 520 28 91   E info@cantillon.be
www.cantillon.be

NOT SO LONG AGO, visiting Cantillon felt like going into an old bonded warehouse, full of musty nooks and crannies and a whole bunch of barrels. Nowadays it feels more like visiting the set of a play that opens in a Sonoma Valley winery. Everything is smartened up – they even have lighting. The barrels remain, of course, along with the essential mustiness, the whiff of microflora in the roof, vital for spontaneous fermentation.

The 'caves' are open to casual visitors every day except Sunday, from 09.00 (10.00 Saturday) to 17.00. A self-guided tour with a helpful guide written in several languages, costs a couple of Euros and includes two samples at the end. More formal tours can be arranged for groups.

There is a sampling area near the entrance, where you can buy beer to try on the premises and also a takeaway facility. Best stock up as and when you can, as production restrictions lead frequently to supplies running dry. Their options to increase production by moving premises are limited by the need to retain the microbiological treasures of the roof spaces.

The staff are helpful but this is a working brewery and distribution centre, so they can get busy with the day job. They are used to strangers wandering around, of all levels of knowledge and interest. They can explain their strange crafts in various languages – this is Brussels after all.

Twice a year – in March and November – there is a public brewing day, starting at 06.00 and running through to mid-evening. This demonstrates the brewing process from the preparation of ingredients through to the first exposure of the freshly brewed beer to the open air.

In recent years brewing days have shifted a week or two closer to Christmas because of climate change – temperatures being critical to spontaneous fermentation.

BREWERY Cantillon

🍷 Cantillon Bruocsella Grand Cru

5% alcohol by volume
Beer style Oude lambic (bottled)
🍾 **37.5** cl & **75** cl bottles
UK importer Belgian Beer Import (Bierlijn); & Shelton Brothers UK
US importer Shelton Brothers

THE CANTILLON BREWERY, based in the most multicultural area of inner Brussels, produces eight regular bottled beers and two draught beers. If this book were a straightforward listing of the 100 best beers made in Belgium all ten would be included. As it is, to balance the book we have chosen only five – a distinction shared only with Dupont (p. 54).

We begin with this rare example of a bottled *oude lambic*. It may look and taste like a gueuze but in fact is unblended, with no refermentation. What a whisky maker might term cask strength, though in this instance it is no stronger than the rest.

TASTING NOTES
The golden colour of this strange beer is deceptive but the absence of a head is telltale. This is undiluted three-year-old lambic. It has a nose of aged oak, of leather-bound volumes in an antiquarian bookshop and of wild mushrooms. The taste gives yet more wood and tannin. Unbelievably, there is some hint of unfermented sweetness underneath all this. And of sherry casks. The finish is made up of all the above, retreating.

VERDICT
Not a beginner's beer. Save it until your palate has begun to accept lambic beers. Even then it helps to taste it under supervision. An ultra-dry, low carbonation, lambic masterpiece.

Brewery information *See p. 33*

Cantillon Fou' Foune

5% alcohol by volume
er style Fruit lambic (apricot)
37.5 cl & 75 cl bottles
mporter Belgian Beer Import (Bierlijn); & Shelton Brothers UK
mporter Shelton Brothers

THE MAN BEHIND the preservation and forceful rejuvenation of the Cantillon brewery was Jean-Pierre Van Roy, a die-hard traditionalist in all things lambic. His uncompromising stances on the proper production of lambic beers have annoyed most of the rest of the Belgian brewing industry, including most other lambic producers. No, make that all other lambic producers.

In truth they all admire him immensely, even when they do not feel they should. As with all controversial characters, it is the incongruities that fascinate most, and this beer is perhaps the most delicious of his creations.

Jean-Pierre is the first to term a lambic stepped with French apricots as 'traditional', adding words to the effect that as lambic is a living beer style, provided one uses real fruit, how does it matter?

TASTING NOTES
Fou' Foune comes with an orangey-gold colour, sporting a slight haze. The nose gives some smoke and a fruity character that is indeed apricot-like, overlying the classical wet-wood and 'horse blanket'. In the taste however, there is little or no apricot or peach but rather something spicy, even meaty. If any fruit is to the fore, it is physalis – or Cape gooseberry. Of course, there is a lot of lactic acid, and this time a little acetic. The mouthfeel is velvety, which is appropriate given the fruit. The finish is sharp.

VERDICT
Unusual both in theory and in practice, though for different reasons.

Brewery information *See p. 33*

Cantillon Iris

5% alcohol by volume

Beer style Gueuze

75 cl bottles only

UK importer Belgian Beer Import (Bierlijn); & Shelton Brothers UK

US importer Shelton Brothers

THE CANTILLON FAMILY opened their brewery in 1900. It was the family business of Jean-Pierre's wife, when he took over in 1978. Control passed to their son Jean in 2003, an altogether more charming man but blessed with the same playfulness.

Part of the appeal of this stoically obstinate company is their willingness to push boundaries when creating new beers, especially if this makes a fool of the existing law. This is one such.

Iris is made entirely from spontaneously fermented beer and tastes for all the world like a great gueuze. However, as it is made entirely from malted barley, it is not legally a lambic or gueuze at all.

The real joke is that the sugary sweet, crystal clear, mass-production, blonde ales dabbed with lambic, sold in every café in Brussels under the name of Gueuze, do qualify, rendering the law useless for consumers.

TASTING NOTES

Iris is a light-amber drink, with an obvious but limited haze. Some yellow and pink highlights shine under a short white head that is prone not to stay. The nose gives lambic again, with fresh hops and sometimes a cheesy odour of old hops, though one recent version seemed to have American hop notes. There is also something fruity in the taste, plus an exotic hardwood that has been dampened. Any bitterness is subdued, giving way to outspoken lactic sourness. The finish is absolutely like old lambic. No more hops here, it is exceedingly dry.

VERDICT

This is a beer brewed and fermented in distinct batches. Thus far every new one seems to have got better. Dry-hopping has complicated the beer marvellously. This road is still being explored. A beer lover's lambic for the 21st century, perhaps.

Brewery information *See p. 33*

Cantillon

Cantillon Lou Pepe Framboise

5% alcohol by volume
style Fruit lambic (raspberry)
       37.5 cl & **75** cl bottles
importer Belgian Beer Import (Bierlijn); & Shelton Brothers UK
importer Shelton Brothers

IT IS A MATTER OF OPINION whether Van Roy senior really retired in 2003 or not. True, he is not around quite as often as previously, but neither has he yet bought a camper van and gone off round the world.

To mark his departure the brewery created a small range of short-run beers, intended as the crème de la crème, and named these Lou Pepe – the name by which the grandchildren knew him.

The three Lou Pepe brands, a gueuze, a kriek and this *framboise*, are made exclusively from two-year-old lambics chosen from the best casks, mainly those in old red Bordeaux wine casks. Fruit is then steeped in these in concentration 50% higher than used in making the ordinary *framboise*, **Rosé de Cantillon**.

TASTING NOTES

An unbelievably deep cherry-red beer swirls in the glass, acquiring a slight brown haze if the sediment is added. Its fleeting, thin head is a deep rosy-red colour. The nose is pure, intense, freshly plucked raspberries. There is just enough room for some wet wood and a waft of chalky blackboard at the back of the fruit. First impressions can be of a light version of some lush, eastern Mediterran- ean, sweet red wine though this taste gives way immediately to wild raspberry, a little subdued, with woody overtones. There is sourness from fruit acids and the slightest hints of lactic and acetic. If one can speak of an aftertaste, this is once more raspberries, lingering on and on. The mouthfeel is a bit sharp and very dry, though not aggressively so. It is extremely refreshing.

VERDICT

This is one of the world's great drinks and a fabulous beer.

Brewery information *See p. 33*

Cantillon Vigneronne

5% alcohol by volume
Beer style Fruit lambic (grape)
37.5 cl & 75 cl bottles
UK importer Belgian Beer Import (Bierlijn); & Shelton Brothers UK
US importer Shelton Brothers

IF LOU PEPE wanted to take his mythical camper van round the world, he would be welcomed by so many craft brewers that accommodation costs would be negligible. With other Belgian brewers guaranteed to chip in the cost of travel and incidentals, he could have a great trip.

The downside is that nobody would be left to justify the impertinence of having created a lambic made with grapes.

TASTING NOTES
The fact that Vigneronne features white Muscat grapes in its production makes this beer's pinkish-speckled, orange-gold colour, under a slight white head, a smaller surprise than may otherwise have been the case. Likewise the nose is malonate, or Muscat de Samos. Far from Muscat, the sour taste brings one onto the correct geographical and organoleptic path. The typical and outspoken Muscat background asserts itself unmistakably. A sharp finish rounds it all off with the grapes giving an oily perfume around the beer.

VERDICT
This wine-beer is a superb concoction, making it an all-time favourite drink and a serious challenge to the standard definition of a beer.

Brewery information *See p. 33*

Caracole

Caracole Ambrée

8% alcohol by volume

beer style Strong amber ale

33 cl & 75 cl bottles and occasionally on draught

importer Belgian Beer Import (Bierlijn)

importer D&V International

BREWERIES ARE A RARITY in the Belgian province of Namur. Charles Debras opened 'The Snail' brewery in 1990, initially in the city of Namur, moving to his current brewhouse in 1994.

This building had been a brewery for two hundred years before closing in 1971. This is currently the best producer in the province, its three other regular beers (**Nostradamus**, **Saxo** and **Troublette**) and their organic 'Bio' versions, being almost as accomplished.

TASTING NOTES

Caracole is a bright amber beer, adorned with a fairly thick, stable, off-white head. The delightful nose has amber malts and caramel, with nutty and herbal touches. The mouth should be shaken alive with caramel, *Amer Picon* liqueur, and a finishing touch of ginger. There should be sweetness, balanced by the spices in the brew. Although stoutly built, the mouthfeel is velvety. On swallowing there is a memory of fried carrots, though what lingers is the spicy-sweet liqueur flavour.

VERDICT

It is impossible not to like all the beers from Caracole – and their unusual labels – with this being the one that stands furthest outside the norm for its style.

Brasserie la Caracole
Côte Marie-Thérèse 86, 5500 Falmignoul
T 082 74 40 80 **F** 082 74 52 58
E info@brasserie-caracole.be
www.brasserie-caracole.be

The brewery is open to the public every Saturday throughout the year from 14.00 to 19.00 and daily in July and August from 13.00 to 19.00. A tour of the brewhouse is de rigueur though you can just as easily visit for a beer in the dark, high-ceilinged, old brick-lined tasting room. Every beer made on the premises, including a couple made by other brewers hiring the brewery's facilities for a day, is available for sampling or take-away.

Brewing at Saint Feuillien

Chimay Grande Réserve

9% alcohol by volume
Beer style Strong abbey-style ale
75 cl bottles only
UK importer James Clay & Sons
US importer Manneken-Brussel Importers

AT THE ABBAYE DE SCOURMONT, in the hamlet of Scourmont, six kilometres south of Chimay in southern Hainaut, they have brewed beer on a small scale since 1862 and commercially since the early 1920s. This beer is in theory the same as blue-top Chimay (or *Bleue*) in 33 cl bottles, though the 75 cl formulation seems to assist the ripening significantly. It derives from what was originally a Christmas beer.

The idea of monks hulking sacks of hops round the brewhouse and tipping them lovingly into copper kettles of boiling wort, guided in their noble art by the hand of God is great for marketing purposes but is sadly squit. In practice, beer produced in the six Trappist breweries of Belgium is made using standard methods and ingredients – they just happen to be made within the walls of a Trappist abbey and under monastic supervision.

The commercial pressures are very different but are nonetheless significant. The purpose of the brewery is to raise money for the Order and its social aims, not to be the subject of charity.

VERDICT

The reputation of Chimay beers have taken quite a pummelling in recent years, which is a shame because they are well-meaning brewers. This is now their best beer, though their Chimay Blanche on draught can be good. TW finds their regular beers more obvious and unrefined than they were. JPP's view is that this is a great beer that was once a magnificent one.

TASTING NOTES

Chimay Grande Reserve presents itself as a deep brown beer under a light brown head. The aroma bursts with roasted sugar-loaded malts, the intense fruitiness of overripe plums and pears and a yeasty backdrop like meat gravy. The taste is bitter from roasted malt rather than the flowers of the hop bine. The heavy character builds gradually. The fine aromas perceived in the nose are coarser in the mouth. The yeast is still there but the fruit is reduced to a little pear and some sweet banana. There is more bitterness at the back of the nose, this time with liquorice and some woodiness. Full bodied and chewy, its high alcohol content is remarkably well hidden.

Bières de Chimay SA – NV
Route de Charlemagne 8, 6464 Baileux
T 060 21 03 11   **E** info@chimay.be   www.chimay.com

The gardens, including the cemetery and the church of the Abbey Notre Dame de Scourmont may be visited (daily 08.00–20.00), but the abbey buildings and brewery may not.

The nearby **Auberge de Poteaupré** (5 Rue de Poteaupré, Scourmont – **T** 060 21 14 33) is a small hotel-restaurant that works with the Abbey. It has a huge dining area and summer terrace, plus a shop selling the Abbey's beers and cheeses. It is always closed on Mondays and usually on Wednesdays too, except in high summer. Other days it opens at 11.00 and closes at 22.00, or 18.00 on weekdays out of season.

Cnudde Bruin (Also known as Louis V)

4.7% alcohol by volume

beer style Aged brown ale

Only found on draught

importer The beers of Cnudde brewery are not exported yet

importer The beers of Cnudde brewery are not exported yet

UNTIL A DECADE AGO the town of Oudenaarde in East Flanders was famed for its stewed and aged brown ales. The method was as traditional as it was time-consuming. This beer is the last brown ale made in the area that still uses aspects of the old techniques, though it was always unique.

When their elderly father, the brewer, died a few years back it was assumed that his three sons, the Cnudde brothers, who all had their own careers, would dismantle the brewery and sell off its pubs. Brewing was down to six times a year and bottling had stopped thirty years back. But with help from the nearby Roman brewery, they are soldiering on, using antique equipment to make an old-fashioned sort of ale.

TASTING NOTES

This dark brown beer has a mossy-green sheen and sports a small brownish head. In the nose, one catches immediately the characteristic tart stamp of lactic acid, with wood and rust.

These are found in the taste too, along with nuances of *drop*, a liquorice sweet found in the Low Countries. The beer is no more than medium bodied. The nice, sourish edge is exactly right astride the sweet base. Some of its flavours are mistaken for cherry.

VERDICT

Very refreshing despite the sweetness. A relic of a bygone age but possibly the herald of a new one. The best reason to get off the train at Eine.

Brouwerij Cnudde
Fabriekstraat 8, 9700 Eine-Oudenaarde
T 055 31 18 34

The brewery is not open for visits. This beer can only be tried at nine cafés in Eine, on the outskirts of Oudenaarde, the nearest to the brewery being the **Casino** (6 Eineplein), which is open from 17.00 on Thursday to Sunday and also from 10.00 to 13.30 at weekends.

Contreras

🍷 Contreras Mars Especial

6.5% alcohol by volume

Beer style   Regional specialty

🍾🛢 **33** cl bottles and occasionally on draught

UK importer Belgian Beer Import (Bierlijn)

US importer The beers of Contreras brewery are not exported to the US yet

UNTIL ABOUT FIVE YEARS AGO, Willy Contreras, bearer of a name that can be traced back to the time when Belgium was the Spanish Netherlands, sat in the brewery his family had owned since 1818, making some really rough but strangely appealing brews, in the best Flemish oud bruin style of yesteryear. Gushing, ferrous, barnyard ales they were, complex and underrated.

Willy always said that his "Maartse" or "Märzen" beer was the best of these because he felt his brewing water 'came into bloom' in March each year, when the beer was made. It probably had more to do with it being bottle-conditioned, unlike the others in those days.

Willy retired and along came son-in-law, Frederik De Vrieze. Confronted with a ramshackle and essentially non-viable brewery that made a couple of lovably eccentric but not hugely successful beers, it was time to take a few decisions. Four years and as many new beers later, the 'new' brewery is still a work in progress.

TASTING NOTES

Nowadays, the newly conjured Mars Especial is a more refined Belgian ale – still off piste but only by a snowball or two. It is a golden-amber beer with a thick, dissipating head. The nose has amber and crystal malts, plus cookies. A sharp, young taste comes through, like concentrated vegetable matter. Its moderate acidity has a faint lactic touch, bringing a mild burning sensation to the mouth. The light to medium body remains from its previous incarnation.

VERDICT

Numerous new beers are appearing from the brewery under the Valeir brand, all to a standard pattern of ale styles. We are hoping that the glorious eccentricity of this beer and of its buddy, **Tonneke**, will not be lost in a sea of conformity. Right now it comes across like an EU-approved novelty. A bit more 'perfect infection' would not go amiss.

Brouwerij Contreras
Molenstraat 115, 9890 Gavere
T 09 384 27 06   **E** info@contreras.be
www.contreras.be

The brewery cannot be visited.
Several cafés are owned in the town of Gavere and its surrounding area but none stands out as a 'must visit'.

De Koninck Amber

5% alcohol by volume
er style Pale ale
On draught, and pasteurised in bottles
mporter James Clay & Sons
mporter Belukus Marketing

DE KONINCK is the Antwerp brewery and De Koninck Amber on tap (Du: *van 't vat*) is the beer of Antwerp. The draught version is known locally by the name of its glass, a *bolleke*. The bottled product has the same recipe and production method as the draught version but is pasteurised, which seems to make a huge difference. We describe only the draught version.

Sadly for Antwerp and for Belgian brewing, the company is struggling with its vision for the future.

TASTING NOTES
De Koninck Amber is an inviting, light-bodied, clear, foxy beer. When poured correctly, which is not in one draw, it sports a luxurious, lacy, yellowish head. While it should be well saturated with CO_2, it ought not to be fizzy. The nose speaks of amber malts, sugar, hops and a tell-tale hint of burned sulphurous rubber, in an overall aroma of fresh grist. The taste should be an ideal balance of malt sweetness and fine hop bitterness, while the CO_2 gives a hint of sourness. Fresh, it has elements of freshly mown grass, though with time a biscuit flavour develops. Aftertaste is not its strong point, though the hop bitterness lasts.

VERDICT
To an Antwerpener (or *Sinjoor*), this is the standard by which all other beers are measured. Never visit Antwerp without drinking one, though not all pubs serve it equally well, so you may need to try several.

Brouwerij De Koninck NV
Mechelsesteenweg 291, 2018 Antwerpen 1
T 03 218 40 48   **F** 03 230 85 19
E info@dekoninck.com
www.dekoninck.be

Guided group visits only, via the website.

De Ryck

De Ryck Special

5.5% alcohol by volume

Beer style Pale ale

On draught and sometimes in **33** cl & **75** cl bottles

UK importer Belgian Beer Import (Bierlijn)

US importer The beers of De Ryck brewery are not exported to the US yet

As with Contreras (p. 44) the De Ryck brewery is a work in progress, though its current transformation began from a very different baseline.

The De Ryck family are highly respected in the Belgian brewing world, for running an honest-to-goodness, successful, local family beer-making firm. They have served their part of East Flanders well since 1886.

Their beers were very much local specialities and found exclusively on draught. Modern times have seen the emergence of their draught beers in bottles, first 75 cl and now 33 cl, which is fine. They have also expanded or transformed their old beer range to create four regular or seasonal beers under the Arend brand, which might also be fine. But they have also added some new sickly sweet fruit beers and got everyone worried.

The beer we list is their original mainstay. 'Special' (Du: *special*; Fr: *spéciale*) beers emerged around 1900. De Ryck's has for many years been among the best, though it was recently supersized from its historic 4.7% abv.

TASTING NOTES

De Ryck Special on draught is an amber beer that gushes to a huge creamy, yellowish head, fed by lively pearling with some unidentified speckled bits. There are hints of orange in the aroma, with citrus leaf and a bit of hop, plus some oxidation in the malts. It has a neutral taste, with some coloured malts, candy sugar and again slight citrus. The back of the tongue may find caramel. On warming, the malt character comes out more strongly. It is light to medium bodied, quite dry, with some stickiness in the mouthfeel. The bottle-conditioned beer has a dryness and alcohol presence that the draught version does not have.

VERDICT

For many years this has been, with **De Koninck Amber** (p.45) the classic draught pale ale of Flanders, a well-made session beer.

[Note: the brewery also makes a slightly darker, stronger Christmas Pale Ale, which we have omitted as in recent years, its hoppy bite is somewhat diminished. Overseas it is Arend Winterbier.]

Brouwerij De Ryck
Kerkstraat 24, 9550 Herzele
T 053 62 23 02   **F** 053 63 15 41
E brouwerij.de.ryck@skynet.be
www.brouwerijderyck.be

Group visits for parties of 15 or more are easy to arrange via the website. The brewery occasionally holds open days and has both a shop and tasting room for private parties.

De Ryck owns numerous cafés in area. Opposite the brewery gates, the **Torenhof** (39 Kerkstraat) is a traditional small town café with a loyal following.

🍷 Arabier

7.8% alcohol by volume

beer style Strong amber ale

🛢 33 cl bottles and occasionally on draught

importer Belgian Beer Import (Bierlijn)

importer B. United International

Kris Herteleer outside the brewery's 'mad' façade

'THE MAD BREWERS' began life in 1980, when the Herteleer family took over the recently deceased Costenoble brewery at Esen, near Diksmuide in West Flanders. Their acquisition occurred just as Belgium was starting to see the emergence of some new microbreweries for the first time in four decades. They have become an important part of Belgium's brewing revival.

Although all the Herteleer brothers were home brewers it was Kris, a talented artist, who emerged as both the architect and the spearhead of the brewing business.

TASTING NOTES

Arabier is a clear, yellow to pale amber beer from which big bubbles feed a strong white head. In younger beer the nose is honeyed, being immediately followed by beautiful fresh hops straight from the sack. On ageing it is more alcoholic, nutty and fungal. A chalky flavour may surprise the unwary before the expected hop flavour comes through, more restrained than in the nose. The finish is citrus but without acidity. The bitterness is, well, chalky, if that makes sense. Fruity flavours abound – apricot, papaya, citrus – plus loads of honey. Fresh hops make a return appearance in the aftertaste. With oxidation, a balance arises of biscuit-like sweetness, lactic and fruity acidity and hoppy bitterness.

VERDICT

Far too complex to be seen as a blond beer, this full-bodied brew is heavy without being syrupy.

Brewery information See p. 49

de Dolle Brouwers

Oerbier

9% alcohol by volume
Beer style Strong brown ale
33 cl bottles and occasionally on draught
UK importer Belgian Beer Import (Bierlijn)
US importer B. United International

OERBIER was the original beer made by Dolle
Brouwers. Just as Picasso had his 'Blue Period',
his 'Rose Period' and so on, so Oerbier has had a
number of incarnations over the last twenty-five
years, though always maintaining its popularity.
It began as tangy and idiosyncratic. Then it was
brewed with yeast from Rodenbach, developing
more of an oud bruin character. More recently it
has been in turns stout-like and then a sweet
strong brown.

TASTING NOTES
Under a big yellowish head, that dwindles before
your eyes, blooms a hazy, rich, chestnut-coloured
beer. It unfolds with a fruity nose loaded with
plum and grape, plus both sweet maltiness and
vinous notes. The flavour starts with a harsh
bitterness from high hopping, plus liquorice.
The underbuild is sweet but rich, with both malt
and a grape-like fruit that stays to the finish.
Nowadays it has an unmistakable alcohol burn
and much fuller body than it has had previously.

VERDICT
Oerbier breaks the first rule of brewing, which is
to be consistent. What it does consistently is to
change its personality with the years, somehow
maintaining its essential qualities. It has never
been dull.

Brewery information *See p. 49*

de Dolle Brouwers

Oerbier Special Reserva

12% alcohol by volume

style: Barley wine

33 cl bottles and occasionally on draught

importer Belgian Beer Import (Bierlijn)

importer B. United International

DOLLE BROUWERS were among the first of the newer breweries to realise the power of the export market to underpin business back home. Their active involvement with their US importers has also led to a number of unexpected developments to their product range.

An **Export Stout** (8%), which TW rates highly but JPP does not, appeared initially for the US market and more recently in Belgium. There has also been a series of *Reserva* beers, fermented over long periods in wine, calvados, sherry or other barrels before bottling. Other Dolle Brouwers beers, like **Stille Nacht** and **Dulle Teve**, have appeared in these forms but this one has been the best.

TASTING NOTES

The 2005 Vintage of Oerbier Reserva is a deep, dark brown, hazy beer under a huge yellow-brownish head. It gives off fumes of grapes, Pineau des Charentes, wine, old wood and wood stain, wafting up with impressions of preserved dark fruit and oranges. Its character is vinous, sporting grapes and raisins, or maybe a special kind of aged fruit brandy. There is a slightly fruity acidity. It is full bodied, with a blatant alcohol burn, yet syrupy. The 2002 Vintage was more amber with a red sheen, coming with a nose of fresh, ripe brambles on sherry, plus a touch of home-made raspberry jam. Intensely fruity, this older beer is sweet and sour in the best West Flanders tradition – plummy with a dash of lactic acid, immensely thick and warming with obvious alcohol.

VERDICT

A superb brew that returns to the past by using Brettanomyces refermentation as conditioning. Thoughtful of the Americans to ask Belgian brewers to return to these older methods.

Brouwerij De Dolle Brouwers
Roeselaerestraat 12b, 8600 Esen
T 051 50 27 81   **F** 051 51 03 37
E info@dedollebrouwers.be
www.dedollebrouwers.be

The brewery is open on Saturdays between 09.00 and 19.00 and Sundays between 14.00 and 19.00. It has a large drinking area in which hang some of brewer Kris Herteleer's paintings.

There is an English language tour of the old brewery at 14.00 every Sunday, often hosted by the formidable Mevrouw Herteleer senior.

Drie Fonteinen

AD Bieren bvba
Hoogstraat 2a, 1650 Beersel
T 02 306 71 03   **F** 02 305 07 41
E info@3fonteinen.be
www.3fonteinen.be

ALTHOUGH BREWERY VISITS must be pre-arranged, anyone can buy beers to take away from the brewery counter, between 09.00 and 19.00 on Fridays and Saturdays all year round, plus Thursdays between April and October.

Armand Debelder is one of the driving forces behind HORAL, the organisation of lambic makers that campaigns for the protection and promotion of traditional lambic beers. Every other year, most of the brewers of HORAL open their doors for a weekend to visitors, which is becoming a sort of pilgrimage for followers of the arts of spontaneous fermentation.

For the rest of the time, by far the best way to sample Drie Fonteinen (3F) beers is at the **Drie Fonteinen** tavern on Beersel's town square (3 Hermann Teirlinckplein – **T** 02 331 06 52; **F** 02 331 07 03) from which the brewery grew. This is closed on Tuesdays and Wednesdays but opens on other days from 10.30 to 22.30.

This locally famous café-restaurant has grown steadily into a renowned institution in its own right, boasting a classic Fifties' design, a good reputation for dining and, almost as an aside, being the brewery tap for 3F. Booking is recommended for Friday and Saturday nights and Sunday lunch and it is closed over Christmas and New Year.

The bar sports a handsome set of handpulls drawing draught lambic, home-prepared faro and *kriekenlambiek*, plus all the available bottled beers in a variety of vintages.

Restaurateur Guido and brewer Armand in the brewery's cellar

 Drie Fonteinen
BREWERY

Drie Fonteinen Oude Geuze Vintage

6% alcohol by volume

beer style Oude gueuze

bottles **37.5** cl & **75** cl bottles

importer Belgian Beer Import (Bierlijn)

importer Shelton Brothers

IN 1953 ARMAND DEBELDER's father, Gaston, moved the family business from the Drie Bronnen (or 'Three Springs') café in Hoogstraat to new premises on the square, which with Flemish flippancy he called the 'Three Fountains'.

With that move came another – the creation of a *geuzestererij*. They bought lambics from other brewers, such as Girardin (p. 66) and Lindemans, and fermented them in caves around the village. Sometimes cherries or raspberries were steeped to make kriek. Others were blended to make an own-brand gueuze.

By the 1990s, most lambic makers were disappearing and it became apparent to Armand that he would soon run out of lambic suppliers. Therefore he set about making his own and in 1999 opened the first new lambic brewery in living memory.

We could have chosen any of the expanding, all-authentic range of gueuzes and fruit beers to come from this excellent small-town family business, but have chosen deliberately to illustrate their excellence with two extreme representatives of a generally excellent range.

TASTING NOTES

The Oude Geuze Vintage is a hazy, grainy-coloured beer with a Chablis-like sheen and a fast-receding whitish head. A fine lemon-citrus nose sits against the classic lambic aroma of 'horse blanket', leather soap, old wood, sulphur, lactic acid, wheat, and in this instance, tarragon. In recent years it has become milder, perhaps as the brewery's own lambics feature more strongly. Its sour, green apple flavours are less prominent while smoked, grainy, near sweet-malty flavours are stronger. There is something of sweet Muscat grape in there too. Better bodied than most gueuzes, it is slick, with a residual sweetness, retaining a sparkling mineral water feel.

VERDICT

If it says 3 Fonteinen on the label, buy it! Do not obsess that it must be Vintage, as all their gueuze beers are usually wonderful. This one is simply a superb effort among many.

Brewery information *See p. 50*

Drie Fonteinen

🍷 Drie Fonteinen Schaarbeekse Kriek

6% alcohol by volume

Beer style Oude kriek

🍾 **75** cl bottles only

UK importer Belgian Beer Import (Bierlijn)

US importer Shelton Brothers

SEPARATING PARTS OF a family business is always likely to be traumatic. This is no more so than when one party wants to do something bizarre, such as planning to open a new lambic brewery because they reckon the world is going to reverse its sixty-year-long trudge away from the only style of beer in the world that routinely takes five years to make.

It has been a long old haul but with a bit of luck the worst is now over. Not that adversity has curbed the desire to experiment. This particular beer comes from a simple idea – make a kriek that uses the originally favoured type of cherry, *Schaerbeekse krieken*.

It was delivering on the idea that was crazy. To find the Schaerbeek cherries nowadays you must visit largely untended orchards that have not been grubbed up to make way for more profitable crops. In many cases the trees had virtually returned to the wild. For this reason it will probably be the last of its kind ever made.

TASTING NOTES

Forget what you thought you knew about the normal colour range for beers. This is the ultimate deep-red, garnet coloured beer, under a dense, cyclamen pink head. It has a downy deposit at its end. The aroma is pure concentrated cherry, as full as the bursting of a fresh, ripe, sour cherry right under your nose. It is superbly tart despite a concentrated, full-cherry flavour, neither sweet nor outspokenly acidic. The lambic underbuild is clearly detectable, but plays second fiddle to the all-conquering fruit. None of this prevents it having a quite vicious acid-burn, relieved by a full, fruity mouthfeel.

VERDICT

Armand Debelder wanted this beer to be a reminder of the past and he has achieved this without question. Sadly, in proving that with determination you can harvest enough real *Schaarbeekse krieken* to bring an old tradition back to life, he also showed that without some brave landowner deciding to plant an uncommercial crop, it will be difficult ever to repeat the experiment.

Brewery information *See p. 50*

52

Dubuisson

Bush Prestige (US name: Scaldis Prestige)

13% alcohol by volume

beer style Barley wine

75 cl bottles only

importer James Clay & Sons

importer B. United International

BRASSERIE DUBUISSON is one of two breweries in the village of Pipaix, in the Hainaut beer belt, east of Tournai. For many years it produced a single 12% abv beer called Bush, the name being an Anglicisation of the family's name, as well as a nod in the direction of acknowledging that this was an English-style amber-coloured barley wine.

In recent years their portfolio has expanded through the creation of beers of lower strength. Bush Prestige on the other hand, manages to move in the opposite direction.

Lengthy legal battles have condemned them to dropping the real name of the beer in all but seven countries of the world. This is because the name upsets the global corporation that makes Bud. Therefore, in the US and elsewhere it gets called Scaldis instead. As the new beers are not at all English we do not see why Dubuisson would not make a perfectly decent name.

TASTING NOTES

Prestige is a hazy amber beer, the high alcohol content of which sees off any serious head. On smelling, the superb alcoholic, liqueur-like aroma is impressive, full of nuts and nearly overripe fruit on alcohol. Its sweetish, alcoholic taste is also fruity. It is strangely delicate but strong, with aspects of cashew nuts and raisins, plus a vinous, woody character. There is a 'wow factor' in its full, brandy-like qualities. Naturally full-bodied, it teeters on the edge of being syrupy. Its aftertaste has a slight presence of incense.

VERDICT

This is hands down the best high-strength, wood-aged beer to come out of Belgium in modern times.

Brasserie Dubuisson Frères sprl
Chaussée de Mons 28, 7904 Pipaix-Leuze
T 069 67 22 21 **F** 069 66 17 27
E info@br-dubuisson.com
www.br-dubuisson.com

Brewery tours can be arranged for groups. We think the regular tours at 15.00 on Saturdays have now ceased.

At the front of the brewery is the **Trolls & Bush** café, an excellent, large, modern café-restaurant that opens every day except Monday, from 11.00 to midnight. The food (12.00–15.00 & 19.00–22.00) is good too. There is a shop selling all the beers including this one.

Brasserie Dupont sprl
Rue Basse 5, 7904 Tourpes-Leuze
T 069 67 10 66 **F** 069 67 10 45
E contact@brasserie-dupont.com
www.brasserie-dupont.com

Group visits by arrangement. Currently the café opposite the brewery (see below) is experimenting with running their own tours, at 14.00 on the third Saturday of the month. We assume brewery director Olivier knows as details are on the brewery website.

On the last weekend of September, as part of a village open day, the brewery, its cheese factory and bakery all open their doors to the public. The brewery's modern kit is housed in one of the most atmospheric farm breweries anywhere.

Opposite the brewery gates, the **Caves Dupont** (8 Rue Basse) is an excellent one-bar village pub with some good movie memorabilia. It opens every day except Wednesday, from 09.30 onwards and stocks most of the Dupont beers, with extra helpings of rural authenticity.

Another local café worth a visit is the **Forge** on the village square (5 Place), the epitome of a village local, Wallonian style.

Dupont first brewed **Cervesia** (p.57) for the Archeosite at Aubechies, originally an Iron Age archaeological dig, in part funded through the sale of this beer. Since 1983 archaeologists have been excavating the area between Aubechies and nearby Blicquy, discovering finds from Neolithic through to Roman times.

Some findings are displayed in a museum at Blicquy, while at Aubechies itself you can visit a faithful reconstruction of Stone Age, Bronze Age, Iron Age and Gallo-Roman homes, open weekdays throughout the year from 09.00 to 17.00 and at weekends between Easter and October from 14.00 to 18.00.

Dupont

🍷 Biolégère

3.5% alcohol by volume

beer style Saison

📦 🛢 **25** cl bottles and occasionally on draught

importer Beer Direct

importer Vanberg & DeWulf

THE RIMAUX-DERIDDER family had been brewing at their farm in the village of Tourpes, in northern Hainaut since 1844. When Alfred Dupont bought the business in 1920, it would be great to say that his main aim was to build a high quality beer business. But this is not true.

The Belgian economy was seriously damaged by the First World War between 1914 and 1918. Once again foreign armies had come to Belgian soil to settle their scores. In 1920, young Belgians seeking a future were looking abroad and Alfred thought that by providing his son Louis with a business to run and develop, he would dissuade him from emigrating to Canada.

Thankfully for beer lovers, this well-aimed bribe worked and Louis and his descendants have since become rather good at beer making.

Dupont is a fabulous brewery. Set in the village of Tourpes in northern Hainaut, among a swathe of craft breweries found between Tournai and Enghien, it not only produces great beers, it also looks the part. It hides many of its operations in traditional farmyard settings and runs additional businesses on site, such as cheese-making and bread-baking. The juxtaposition of high technical specification, adherence to old-fashioned values and respect for the local environment is great to see.

It was inevitable that Dupont would join the move towards creating organic beers, which are set to have a great future, especially as the Bio brands begin to match their regular equivalents in quality.

Historically saisons were far less strong than today. Just as many mild ales in Britain were popular with those who tilled the fields and stoked the furnaces years ago, so many saisons will have been light and hoppy Belgian equivalents.

Biolégère is probably a more authentic recreation of this classic western Hainaut style than its esteemed big brother (p. 59).

TASTING NOTES

Biolégère is a very pale yellow, hazy beer, under a huge, fine, faintly yellow head. There are wafts of wet cardboard, yet at the same time the spicy, herbal aromas of Dupont yeast. The taste is delicately spicy and the spritzy mouthfeel pleasant but light. Flowery flavours round off the oral impression, ending on a light bitterness. This is no low alcohol variant on proper beer made by chemically removing the ethanol. This is proper light beer, light-bodied but certainly not lightweight.

VERDICT

Although Belgium is famed for its stronger beers, a few excellent lighter beers are produced too. This is probably the best of these.

Brewery information *See p. 54*

BREWERY Dupont

🍷 Bons Vœux

9.5% alcohol by volume

Beer style Barley wine

🍾 🛢 37.5 cl & 75 cl bottles and occasionally on draught

UK importer Beer Direct

US importer Vanberg & DeWulf

THE FULL NAME OF THIS BEER is 'Avec les Bons Vœux de la Brasserie Dupont' or 'With the Best Wishes of Dupont Brewery'. It dates from 1970, when the Dupont family thought it would be a good idea to brew a Christmas present for their best customers. They repeated this year on year and eventually the brew gained cult status.

TASTING NOTES
Bons Vœux is another Dupont beer that can open with explosive gushing, to pour with a huge but unstable white head on top of a hazy, pale peach-orange beer. Barnyard and earthy aromas abound, as well as leather, citrus zest, faint spices and fresh white bread with nuts. Earthy, leaf mould flavours are underpinned by a faint sweetness and soft, lemony, lactic acidity. Background flavours feature wheat-like grain and discreet spices. The beer manages to refresh despite its full, chewy mouthfeel. There is an oily sensation, consistent with an aroma of walnut oil.

VERDICT
The draught version can sometimes be a tad less impressive and give a thinner impression, the bottled version gives new meaning to the idea of a complex, layered beer.

Brewery information See p. 54

Cervesia

8% alcohol by volume

er style Regional specialty

 Mainly **75** cl bottles but occasionally in **25** cl bottles and on draught

importer Beer Direct

importer Vanberg & DeWulf

THE DUPONT thumbprint comes from a complex yeast mix said to involve six strains. It also uses an above average hop presence in most of its beers. The exception is this one, which has very few hops at all, relying instead on an authentic spice recipe used in old Celtic beverages, researched by the brother-in-law of the former brewer.

Before the advent of the hop a combination of herbs and spices, called *gruut* in Old Dutch, was used as a preservative. The *gruut* merchants of Bruges held such power in mediaeval times that small wars were fought to gain control of their business.

TASTING NOTES

Cervesia's golden colour excels, presenting only the slightest haze, crowned by a small, slowly diminishing rim of foam. It is medium to full bodied. Nowadays it has a perfumed, even soapy nose, different from previous years, when it was spicier. On the other hand, it retains its citrus, peppery, grains of paradise and cookie (bottom-of-the-pie) tastes, swinging again to a perfumed finish and on to a spicy aftertaste. Maybe this is normal for a *gruut* beer – who knows?

VERDICT

Even more so than with the **Biolégère** (p. 55), we wrestled with whether or not to include this beer. Its place in brewing history and its excellence recommended it but it was until recently very scarce. However, specialist beer cafés in Belgium are starting to stock it as an oddity, so we were finally convinced.

Brewery information *See p. 54*

🍷 Moinette Blonde

8.5% alcohol by volume

Beer style Tripel

🍾 🛢 33 cl, **75** cl & **150** cl bottles and on draught

UK importer Beer Direct

US importer Vanberg & DeWulf

THE TWO MOINETTE BRANDS – the **Brune** is perfectly passable too – arrived in 1955, and this one is Dupont's top seller in Belgium. 'Moine' is a French word for monk and with the beer being called Abbaye de Moinette until 1980, many assumed this was a deliberate attempt to brew an abbey-style tripel.

In fact the name came from the 'Cense de la Moinette', a mill that was part of the original family holding. This had taken its name from 'Pays de Moinette', which in turn had derived from 'moëne', an old French word for 'mire'. The name of the local area at that time had been, roughly, 'Bog Country'. Moinette Blond is, however, anything but a bog standard beer.

TASTING NOTES

Moinette Blonde has a pale orange, peachy colour, a very slight haze, and a slim white head. It has a spicy nose, with pepper, grains of paradise, subdued coriander and some citrus zest, with lavender at the back. The taste is again spicy, with pepper again and grapefruit, perfumed by gentle wafts of coriander when warmer. Dry yet full-bodied, with alcohol clearly there, all the classical features of a good strong ale.

VERDICT

If you must spice a beer then this is how you do it – as a subtle enhancement to a well-made brew. A classic of its kind – the best of the southern strong blondes. Again, a beer best taken from a 75 or 150 cl bottle, as the yeast dynamics appear to give it an extra degree of sophistication.

Brewery information *See p. 54*

Saison Dupont

6.5% alcohol by volume

beer style Saison

33 cl & **75** cl bottles and on draught

importer Beer Direct

importer Vanberg & DeWulf

HAINAUT IS THE HOME of saison beers. Just as the brewers of old Flanders preserved their beers by ageing them in huge oak casks and the brewers of Payottenland did it by a combination of aged, flavourless hops and the ultimate in slow fermentation, the brewers of Hainaut, and possibly Limburg too, chose to use high dose preservatives, or hops if you prefer. These properties were particularly helpful in high summer, or in the season (Fr: *saison*).

TASTING NOTES

Saison Dupont can explode into your glass in more ways than one. Atop a hazy orange beer comes a mass of slightly yellow foam. It yields a fresh nose, lemony, but with some cork-mouldy smell at first. Then a soft cheese aroma as from Brie. It is bitter, tart and orange rind flavoured. A bit bread-yeasty, too. Even relatively well-aged examples show no oxidation or Madeira notes, perhaps because of the hop presence. It is spicy in taste yet no spices are used to make this classic brew. The mouth burns slightly but the beer is dry and refreshing. Seriously bitter in aftertaste, this seems to go beyond hop-bitterness. At the end, again, some earth-cork taste.

VERDICT

Depending on your point of view, Saison Dupont is either the last or the first of the great saisons. It comes in many formats but we recommend the traditional 75 cl champagne bottle size, built for sharing. Surprisingly it makes a great session beer. Just as you think its bitterness will be too much, it proves it can tempt you to just one more.

Brewery information *See p. 54*

Inside the Duvel Moortgat warehouse (see p. 63)

BREWERY # Duvel Moortgat

🍷 Duvel

8.5% alcohol by volume

Beer style   Strong blond ale

   33 cl & **75** cl bottles and occasionally **150** cl & **300** cl bottles

UK importer   James Clay & Sons

US importer   Duvel USA

FOUNDED IN 1871 as a farmhouse brewery in the days when Breendonk, near Antwerp, was surrounded by farmland. The Moortgat family still have a large influence, though it is now one of the most successful public companies for its size in Belgium.

Strongly against the global trend in the food and drink sector generally, and brewing in particular, as the company has grown its products have remained pretty good. Not much dumbing down here, in the older brands at least.

The 'modern' brewhouse completed in 1971 is simply not big enough to deal with its success and a newer, much larger one is planned. That will be the testing time for this ultramodern but still quite traditional company.

Technically the beer should be Duvel Rood (or 'Red') as there remains a flimsier, filtered version on the market called **Duvel Groen** (or 'Green') from way before such an epithet suggested organic – which it is not, currently.

Brewery information   See p. 63

TASTING NOTES

There can be few beers of this strength that are as pale as Duvel. Light yellow-golden in colour, with a greenish sheen, it sports a ridiculously huge white head that leaves classical lace rings. You can be forgiven for mistaking its appearance as a strong lager, yet of course with this flavour it must be an ale. The nose comes with grain, alcohol, dry candy sugar (whatever brewers say about it being odourless) and discreet garden weeds. In the taste, again the candy sugar thumbprint emerges, dry initially then creamier. The silken-smooth finish and velvety palate are what makes this a great beer. The alcohol is hidden to some extent but there is detectable steel under this velvet. The aftertaste is bone-dry with candy sugar, and slightly grassy.

VERDICT

This beer is a classic strong ale that has spawned imitators but no superiors and one that made Belgian strong ales world-famous.

Maredsous 8

8% alcohol by volume

er style Dubbel

33 cl & **75** cl bottles and occasionally on draught

mporter James Clay & Sons

mporter Duvel USA

THE BENEDICTINE ABBEY of Maredsous is set in a particularly attractive part of the Namuroise Ardennes. Unlike the Trappist abbeys it does not brew its own beers but rather lends its name to three beers in exchange for a commission, which funds the abbey, the Order and its charitable works.

These semi-detached arrangements often work out rather badly for the consumer. Commercial breweries exploit the religious connection for all it is worth but make rather naff beers sold mainly on image. The Maredsous brands are an honourable exception, all three (there is also a 6% abv blond and a 10% abv barley wine) being not only excellent but also subject to regular improvement.

TASTING NOTES

Maredsous 8 presents as a clear, deep red-brown beer under a brown-tinted head. The nose is fruity, with peach, prune, dark cherry and red grapes, and full of esters. The immediate taste is again fruity and sweet from a solid malt base, rolling on into the smokiness of a good cigar. There is some hop bitterness, but at the same time an aroma of cypress trees. The mouthfeel features alcohol, but restrained, accommodating a warm, full body. That cigar flavour lingers as an aftertaste, with hints of different fruits, now all blended together, cleverly balanced.

VERDICT

An excellent example of the Moortgat range of abbey beers, which challenge the Trappist breweries on quality.

[TW NOTES: personally I rate the mountainous Maredsous 10 even higher – a small amber-orange miracle.]

Brouwerij Duvel Moortgat NV
Breendonkdorp 58, 2870 Breendonk-Puurs
T 03 886 94 00   **F** 03 886 46 22   **E** info@duvel.be
www.duvel.be

Group tours are fairly easy to arrange, and now end in the new visitor centre.

Fantôme

Fantôme Black Ghost

8% alcohol by volume

Beer style Strong brown ale

75 cl bottles only

UK importer Belgian Beer Import (Bierlijn)

US importer Shelton Brothers

DANY PRIGNON's Fantôme brewery has been operating since 1988 and its products have divided beer lovers from the word go. Some people – usually Belgians – hate the beers with a vengeance and cannot say a decent word about them. Others – more often foreigners – praise them to high heaven. The problem is, at least in part, inconsistency. While some of the beers are little marvels, others can be disappointing.

TASTING NOTES

Black Ghost is dark brown, highly hazy and crowned with a slim rim of yellowish foam. In the nose, we have a classical aroma of cypress trees and fresh juniper, the spice of English gin, often found in those Wallonian brews that contain a lot of dark malts and dark candy sugar. The taste gives another sensation with flavours like blueberry, myrtle and bog-myrtle signposting enormous depths full of strange and rare malts. It is very full-bodied as well as feeling potent.

VERDICT

Love them or hate them, you cannot ignore Fantôme beers, for this book we have chosen one that is a consistent performer, and has been produced in pretty much the same way several times. On top form, this beer is amazing.

Brasserie Fantôme
Rue Préal 8, 6997 Soy
T&F 086 47 70 44   **E** contact@fantome.be
www.fantome.be

The brewery, which is in a village near the Ardennaise market town of Hotton, opens at weekends, and daily during school holidays, from 10.30, or whatever. You take the small, ramshackle old farm building on what passes for the main road, as you find it. Their current beers will be for sale to try on the premises or take away. There may be cheese and dry sausage also.

64

Girardin

Girardin Oude Gueuze 1882

6% alcohol by volume

er style Oude gueuze

37.5 cl & 75 cl bottles

nporter Belgian Beer Import (Bierlijn)

nporter D&V International

THE GENIUS OF GIRARDIN is unlikely to be accidental, yet they do little or nothing to shout about it. For years they have confused drinkers by producing a filtered, young, rather ineffectual gueuze in a white-labelled bottle, only recently calling it by a subtly different name. They do not yet produce an oude kriek either.

And as for secrecy, let us say simply that no beer writer either of us knows has ever set foot in its hallowed farm buildings.

TASTING NOTES

Girardin's black label gueuze is a golden-coloured beer with slight orangey highlights. It has a remarkably stable head, dirty-yellow in colour. Close your eyes and you can imagine the stable yard, the late summer grain harvest, freshly cut straw, and the apple store. The immediate impression on tasting is dryness, yet the carbonisation is pretty lively. Together with the tannin, the onslaught on the front teeth is something akin to a dentist's assault on tartar. The real taste arrives retronasally, delivering citrus, pineapple, green apple, lime and lactic acid. Yet there is a slight strain of sweetness, as in the hard, grainy Belgian *speculoos* biscuit. The mouthfeel is undistinguishable from the taste.

VERDICT

This is the experience of the Payottenland outback in a bottle. Considered by many both within and outside the lambic brewing trade to be the ultimate Payottenland gueuze.

Brewery information *See p. 66*

Girardin Oude Lambic

6% alcohol by volume
Beer style Oude lambic (draught)
On draught only
UK importer This beer is never exported
US importer This beer is never exported

THE POPULARITY of lambic beers had been on the wane even before the Second World War engulfed Belgium for the first half of the 1940s. Thereafter, the rush for cheap calories and all things sugary contributed in large part to their even faster decline.

There were a few brewers making lambic beers on an industrial scale. Many of the producers were still based on the farms where their small-scale operations had begun, as a sideline. So it was with Girardin, who by 1990 were one of only nine remaining companies creating drinks based on spontaneously fermented beers.

Occasionally lambic beers can be found in their natural state, on draught. Unlike cask-conditioned ales, such as British 'real ale', draught lambics undergo only gentle fermentation in the barrel. Thus they present with low carbonation – or 'flat', if you prefer. Those cafés that still sell draught lambics often decant them first.

A cask lambic that is six to twelve months old is invariably referred to as young (Du: *jonge*) while those of two years ageing and above are termed old (Du: *oude*). Between the two it is a matter of judgement. Some lambics ripen and mature faster than others.

This beer has been seen in bottled form occasionally in recent times. We infer that the brewery is experimenting with this in the wake of Cantillon's success with **Bruocsella Grand Cru** (p. 34).

TASTING NOTES
This beer should be completely clear. After all it has had two or three years to settle. The colour is that of old sherry. Unsurprisingly, it offers no head at all. The nose is not overwhelming, but Brettanomyces and cheesy hops tell the stranger immediately of its pedigree. The nose too is sherried. As to the taste, think in terms of the great tastes of aged, semi-sweet wines, with even a touch of Muscat grape. Strangely enough, there is still a touch of sweetness, at odds with the dry, tart mouthfeel.

VERDICT
Old lambic is an acquired taste, as are so many of the world's most interesting consumables. Girardin Oude Lambic is shocking, and as such is a classic of its kind. Unsurprisingly it features in the construction of many of the best authentic gueuzes, lending it a strange familiarity to well-travelled palates.

Brouwerij Girardin
Lindenbergstraat 10–12, 1700 Sint-Ulriks-Kapelle
T&F 02 452 94 19

No website, no e-mails and no visits. However, you can turn up to buy beer from their shop every day except Sunday, 08.00 to 12.00 and 13.00 to 18.00 (15.00 Saturday).

Glazen Toren

🍷 Canaster Winterscotch

8.5% alcohol by volume

er style Scotch ale

🍾 **75** cl bottles only

mporter Belgian Beer Import (Bierlijn)

mporter B. United International

In 1988, the new Town Clerk of Aalst in East Flanders, Dirk de Pauw, met for the first time one of the Aldermen, Jef van den Steen. They discovered they were both teachers by background and that they shared a passion for beer. They began home brewing together and eventually enrolled on a three-year brewing course at one of the colleges in Ghent.

By 2004 they had joined forces with a third teacher-cum-beer-nut, had bought a second hand brewing installation and set up a makeshift brewery near Jef's home. January 2007 saw a small but swanky new purpose-built installation and the quality of their four, carefully concocted ales begin to get even better.

TASTING NOTES

Glazen Toren's winter offering sports a good, creamy, beige head that is fast gone, over a deep dark brown beer. There are liquorice, cinnamon and malts in the nose. Tasting reveals it to be sweet, with a blend of spices, plus some fruitiness, maybe sweetened figs or prunes. Still there are some bitter notes, not hoppy, but rather appearing as vegetable. The body is medium, with a slick mouthfeel. The spiciness builds up gradually but never to the point of dominating the beer.

VERDICT

Neither of us normally goes for liquorice-flavoured beers, but this one stands out as a fine winter brew. The brewery's other beers are progressing well too.

BVBA Kleinbrouwerij De Glazen Toren
Glazentorenweg 11, 9420 Erpe-Mere
T&F 053 83 68 17 **E** info@glazentoren.be
www.glazentoren.be

Groups tours by arrangement through the website. The brewery also opens for beer sales every Saturday from 10.00 to 12.00 and 14.00 to 16.00

BREWERY **Hanssens**

Hanssens Artisanaal Oude Geuze

6% alcohol by volume

Beer style Oude gueuze

37.5 cl & **75** cl bottles

UK importer Belgian Beer Import (Bierlijn)

US importer B. United International

THE FACT THAT Hanssens no longer brews lambic beers is all the fault of Kaiser Wilhelm and the invading forces of the Imperial German Army in 1914. They found that breweries were a rich source of copper, which was much in demand in the construction of shells and other weapons of war. In Hanssens' case, this put paid to forty years of brewing.

This setback did not stop them taking in other people's lambics and blending these to make an excellent gueuze, or steeping cherries to make their own kriek.

Brewery information *See p. 69*

TASTING NOTES

Hanssens is a well-carbonated, hazy, orange-amber gueuze, sporting a white head that disappears almost as soon as it is formed. Outspoken 'horse blanket' and citrus define the nose, with aromas of grapefruit peel, lactic acid and damp oak. The taste is tart without making it to really sour. There is a lactic-lemony rind around a full mouthfeel, plus a hint at an unlikely malt sweetness. Complex flavours of Belgian *speculoos* biscuit, wood and tannin abound, signalling its sharper finish. Refreshing it might be, but light bodied it is not.

VERDICT

A quintessential gueuze from the oldest of the true blenders, with complexity the dominant property.

Hanssens

Hanssens Artisanaal Oudbeitje

6% alcohol by volume

er style Fruit lambic (strawberry)

37.5 cl & **75** cl bottles

mporter Belgian Beer Import (Bierlijn)

mporter B. United International

THIS OLD GUEUZE BLENDER has come in for some stick over the years. Although firmly entrenched at the traditional end of the lambic blenders' spectrum – they use only 100% lambic in their beers – they get accused, rightly or wrongly, of using sweeteners and fruit pulps in their fruit beers.

Making this particular beer was like putting out fire with gasoline. If God had meant man to steep strawberries in lambic, He would have given them stones, surely?

TASTING NOTES

The bottle sports a beautiful, stuck solid yeast sediment beneath a peach-coloured beer. There is no head of which to speak. Some sulphur compounds hit the nose along with the familiar 'horse blanket' and oak. Generally it is dominated by a fine fruit aroma that seems to hover between raspberry and strawberry. The taste decides it – unmistakably strawberry, though maybe just suggested by the label. A lemony aroma results in an exotic fruit flavour, again not readily identifiable. The necessary acidity is subdued, but on warming up there is some acetic present, plus sulphur in the mouth. At the back of the nose, blue cheese comes first and, on warming, a less pleasing solvent effect. The mouthfeel is refreshing, thanks to the acidity and carbonation, though the saturation seems less than expected. At the finish is some oak, making it tart but not puckeringly sour.

VERDICT

We know we will upset some lambic aficionados by including this beer in our top 100. OK, strawberries are not a traditional lambic steeper's fruit but taste it and see what you think. Respect for tradition is an acknowledgement that the things that survive longest may well have innate value. It should not exclude new ideas.

Jean Hanssens' daughter Sidy and husband John enjoying a glass of Oudbeitje, a lambic steeped with strawberries.

Hanssens Artisanaal
Vroenenbosstraat 15, 1653 Dworp
T&F 02 380 31 33
E hanssens.artisanaal@proximedia.be
www.proximedia.com/web/hanssens.html

Hanssens' front of house opens to the public for off sales on Fridays from 08.00 to 17.00 and Saturdays from 08.00 to 14.00.

Hanssens were founder members of HORAL and take part in its bi-annual 'open weekend' (see Drie Fonteinen p. 50).

Tuns of lambic ripening in the cellars at Hanssens Geuzestekerij (see p. 69)

Hofblues

5.5% alcohol by volume

Beer style Stout

33 cl & **50** cl bottles

UK importer Belgian Beer Import (Bierlijn)

US importer The beers of 't Hofbrouwerijke brewery are not exported to the US yet

WE IMAGINE THAT by the time this book appears, Jef Goetelen will either have decided that becoming a brewer had been the first warning sign of impending madness, or else will be starting to reap the rewards of a lot of hard work spent perfecting a range of eight beers and planning how to turn an interest into a business.

For now, let us just say that his life is busy. Since his brewery opened south east of Antwerp in 2005, he has managed to put together some interesting beers of great potential, of which this one is for now the best, in our view.

TASTING NOTES

Poured from its stoppered bottle, a dense head in dirty beige looms over a pretty much black beer. Unsurprisingly, the nose is archetypal porter with a touch of sweetness, dark roasted graininess and something a touch salty. The taste is that of a sweeter version of Guinness, but much more lively and ending on a liquorice flavour. It turns out to be well-bodied for a beer of only medium strength.

VERDICT

In all, a nice, lightish stout, with a marked grainy taste. Hopefully a sign of greater things to come.

't Hofbrouwerijke
Hoogstraat 151, 2580 Beerzel
T 015 75 77 07   **E** info@thofbrouwerijke.be
www.thofbrouwerijke.be

No brewery visits are possible.
In the town, the most reliable outlet for the beers is the **Dorp** café (8 Jan de Cordesstraat).

Kerkom

BREWERY

Brouwerij Kerkom
Naamsesteenweg 469
3800 Kerkom-Sint-Truiden
T 011 68 20 87
E info@brouwerijkerkom.be
www.brouwerijkerkom.be

From the outside, the Kerkom brewery looks like any of the other old-established farmsteads that act as brick-built scenery that makes up the backdrop for driving through rural Belgium, in this case along the N80 between the Limburg towns of Gingelom and Sint Truiden. Park up and enter its courtyard and you find a classic square design, with old farm buildings facing inwards away from the weather.

How it differs from all the others is that the buildings on the south side of the yard house a delightfully simple microbrewery that produces some of the best pale ales in Belgium. On the north side is a pleasant summer bar, open every day except Monday, from April to October between 12.00 and 19.00, serving a large terrace.

The real treat is hidden in the old farmhouse, on the side next to the main road. On Saturdays and Sundays from November to March, visitors arriving between 13.00 and 19.00 can enjoy the recreation of a rustic brown café, with a tiled floor, ancient bar fittings, a piano, a stove, a collection of breweriana and a lot more.

This is very much a family business, revolving around a small number of people. Its popularity, while welcome, can mean they get rushed off their feet at busy times. Nonetheless, strike it lucky and you may get a chance to look round the brewery with one of the crew.

Bink Blond

5.5% alcohol by volume

Beer style   Blonde ale

33 cl & **75** cl bottles and on draught

UK importer   Belgian Beer Import (Bierlijn)

US importer   Shelton Brothers

FARMHOUSE BREWERIES were once a regular feature of the Belgian landscape. Many of the remaining independent breweries can trace their origins back to the family farm. There was a small brewery at Kerkom as early as 1878 but this closed in 1968.

When Jean Clerinckx restarted brewing in 1988, on the site where his ancestors had brewed, Limburg was well behind in the Belgian craft beer revival.

Both the setting of the brewery and the beers made there so impressed brewer Marc Limet and his wife Marina Siongers, that when the chance came to take over in 1999, they jumped at it – swallowing hard when they realised what they had taken on. Nearly a decade later, they have spearheaded a revival of self-respect in Limburg brewing.

It is a matter of opinion whether there is a legitimate Limburg style of pale ale that bears some similarity to the saison beers of northern Hainaut. JPP does not believe a word of it. If there is, then it had survived over the years in the form of **Martens Sezoens** (p.79), and has nowadays blossomed through its finest example, Bink Blond.

TASTING NOTES

The beer is orange-yellow, displaying a slight haze. A dense white head, not very stable, crowns the liquid. In the nose, we detect honey and malty syrup, as well as citrus notes. There is no mistaking the bitter taste, though nowadays this is more citrus peel bitterness at first than pure hops. This still leaves it quite refreshing. In the aftertaste we get more hops and, I persuade myself, the flavour of pie – with preserved slices of lemon or oranges – either way, really perfumed. This is a medium-bodied brew, with a long citrus aftertaste.

VERDICT

This is already a superb beer. However, it is also 'a work in progress' as Marc Limet is forever tinkering with it, deliberately trying to make it the beer that speaks for Limburg. Hoppy but beautifully balanced, this is one you buy by the case.

Brewery information   *See p. 73*

Kerkom Reuss

5.8% alcohol by volume
er style Regional specialty
33 cl & 75 cl bottles and on draught
mporter Belgian Beer Import (Bierlijn)
mporter Shelton Brothers

A LITTLE KNOWN FACT about commercial brewing is that it was commonplace over the centuries for brewers to mix their beers. In Flanders, where the range of styles available for blending is far broader, the options available were naturally far broader. One common style was a mix of pale ale with lambic.

The first blend of this unusual revival of an old beer type had a large portion of **Girardin Lambic** (p. 66) and was mainly seen on draught. The second blend, from 2006–07, exists bottled as well, and has more **Kerkomse Tripel** (p. 76) in it, making it delectable if a tad explosive.

Brewery information *See p. 73*

TASTING NOTES
A pale beer with a greenish sheen, lodged under quite a yellow head. The nose reveals the Brettano-myces and lactic acid. The first beer blended had an additional metallic aroma – possibly copper – that was all but gone in the second blend. The taste manages some hop bitterness, alien to lambic, with a little sourness that is out of place in most ales. The second blend has a flavour of green not-quite-ripe grapes, and is yeastier. A medium-bodied beer with a dry finish.

VERDICT
A rather different kind of beer, being more refreshing than the average ale but nowhere as near to the edge as a classic lambic. A worthy renewal of an old tradition.

Kerkom brewer Marc Limet pours a glass of Reuss, a beer that revives an old tradition of mixing ale and lambic.

BREWERY Kerkom

🍷 Kerkomse Tripel (US name: Bink Triple)

9% alcohol by volume
Beer style Tripel
75 cl bottles only
UK importer Belgian Beer Import (Bierlijn)
US importer Shelton Brothers

MARC LIMET makes no secret of the fact that blond beers are his first love in brewing. So when he decided to expand the brewery's range to include a tripel, he allowed himself to experiment with different versions.

Of course the problem when you are an excellent beer maker is that you may make two or more different versions that are equally good. So though we list the Kerkomse (or Bink) version, you may prefer the slightly sweeter, marginally less hoppy **Adelardus**.

TASTING NOTES

This agreeable looking orange-gold beer has only a small head, though it leaves lacy traces. It has a dry nose with a tinge of candy sugar and hops from, possibly, dry hopping. What is really dry is the taste, being virtually free of residual sweetness despite a feeling that it is less attenuated than most tripels. In fact it feels fairly well-bodied. Only in the palate does a dab of sweetness appear. A typically hoppy retronasal aroma stresses the inclination of this beer.

VERDICT

One for those whose want to learn the difference between a well-hopped beer and a highly hopped beer. This is the former.

Brewery information See p. 73

Loterbol

Loterbol Bruin

8% alcohol by volume

er style Strong brown ale

33 cl bottles and on draught

importer Belgian Beer Import (Bierlijn)

importer Shelton Brothers

THE COMPANY THAT is responsible for much of the national and international distribution of Trappist beers, Weynants, based in Diest in Flemish Brabant, had run its own occasional brewery since about 1995, calling it Duysters. For many years the beer quality, like the name of its products and the frequency with which it brewed were all a bit haphazard.

Then something changed, including the building of a new and much larger brewhouse in 2002, and in the way that sometimes the ugliest children can grow into beautiful young adults, Duysters brewery became Loterbol and started sprouting some altogether nicer and more confident beers. This is the one that we think is currently the best.

TASTING NOTES
Loterbol Bruin is a deep, dark brown beer with a reddish sheen, under a canopy formed by a fine, dark, thick, lace-strewing head. Treat the bottle with some care if you want to avoid flunky UFOs. The nose is of dark malts, roasted barley, and sweat. The taste begins as pure walnut, with both the sweetness of the nut and the bitterness of its peel, later turning more to the typical slight acidity of roasted barley. It is well-bodied but certainly not chewy. Stout-like but without any real obligation to a particular style.

VERDICT
An interesting beer with enough improvement in recent years to warrant a rung near the bottom of our demanding ladder.

Café-Brouwerij Loterbol
Michel Theysstraat 58a, 3290 Diest
T 013 32 36 28
www.loterbol.be

Despite the fact that this is the only brewery in Belgium to refer to itself as a 'café-brewery', the café itself only opens on the first Saturday of the month, from 16.00 till midnight. We have no idea why that is.

🍷 Malheur Dark Brut Noir

12% alcohol by volume

Beer style Barley wine

75 cl bottles only

UK importer Cave Direct

US importer Belukus Marketing

THE DE LANDTSHEER family, although brewers in years gone by, had been drinks merchants at the time they decided to create a new brewery in 1997. They began with some blissfully simple ales of varying strengths and then in 2001, brought the world a blond beer that was the first ever made using a process similar to the *méthode Champenoise*.

We must avoid implying that these beers are in any way associated with the fizzy wines of Epernay, as the makers of those efforts get huffy if one tries to trade off their creation. So let us be clear – these are unmistakably strong ales of a fabulous beery character.

By coincidence, Malheur's first such beer came out at virtually the same time as a second Belgian brewer had clearly just had the same completely original thought and produced their very own completely unChampagne-like ale. Amazingly, this was the brewer from the other end of Buggenhout, a town with a population of fewer than ten thousand people. Whoever would have thought that possible?

Thankfully the rival was a bit of a powder puff compared to the Malheur's **Brut Blond**. But just to make the point the brewery went on to produce this blockbuster too.

TASTING NOTES

The Champagne-type bottle opens with a slight gushing for, in the end, very little head. The beer is deep dark brown with a red sheen. Woody, vinous, fruity (plum, fig and bramble) aromas waft up, with some walnut. So what of the taste? This reveals a tannin-rich bitterness covering truckloads of malt. There is a little chocolate flavour, probably thanks to chocolate malt. It is full-bodied and at the edge of syrupy. Finally a long, sweet aftertaste sets in, where full-on mocha emerges.

VERDICT

This tends to be an expensive beer but it is a real treat. And in such a beautiful bottle it looks great next to the Christmas tree. Even better when arranged in a circle of a dozen.

[TW NOTES: At a head-to-head tasting in the early days of production I preferred Malheur's Brut Blond, though I bow to JPP's view that the blonde ale may have bent in the direction of its inferior rival a little and taken on some odd additional flavours. Hence this beer is preferred – though please do not let this put you off trying both.]

Malheur Bieren
Mandekensstraat 179, 9255 Buggenhout
T 052 33 39 11   **F** 052 34 25 28   **E** info@malheur.be
www.malheur.be

Groups visits by arrangement via the website.

Sezoens Blond

6% alcohol by volume

beer style Blonde ale

33 cl bottles and on draught

importer Cave Direct

importer Sezoens Blond is not exported to the US yet

THIS BEER scraped in by the skin of its teeth and more by dint of its historical and possible future role in Belgian brewing than by its current merits. A bottle-conditioned version, called **Opus**, is said to be available at the brewery's private museum but as neither author has ever tasted it – and we have been round the block more often that most – it was not included.

Martens is in many ways a company that is pivotal to the future of the Belgian brewing industry. Founded in 1758, it is both one of the oldest and largest independent breweries in the country. However, it has focused its considerable efforts in recent years on the supermarket brand lager market, creating the sort of dull pap that appeals to mass taste. This has been at the expense, thus far, of its more characterful brands.

This dreary pastime nearly cost it the whole business, when a change in the German government's 'green strategy' rendered its cheap disposable bottles illegal in one of its principle markets.

Sezoens was for many years the (small, hand-held) flag waver for a style of light-coloured, crisp and hoppy Limburg pale ales, of the type beautifully revived by Kerkom and others. Yet far from joining in the revival, this charging bull of a company appears to have let others reap the benefit while they concentrate on the serious business of making the brewing equivalent of white sliced bread.

TASTING NOTES

Sezoens is a yellow-straw coloured, crystal clear beer under a fluffy, disparate head. A grainy, slightly sweet-smelling nose sets one up for the initial taste of sweet grain, malts and a little chaff. Even when there is no visible carbonation, the beer sports prickly fizz. The palate begins fruity, like pineapple, gradually drying to end near bitter. It is medium-bodied.

VERDICT

This beer is not an explosive flavour bomb on steroids. It might be called discreet, though not as discreet as its marketing or distribution, which makes it awkward to find outside northern Limburg. It remains nonetheless a generous, if basic beer, for those who are open to its intricacies.

Brouwerij Martens NV
Reppellerweg 1, 3950 Bocholt
T 089 47 29 80   **F** 089 47 29 84
E info@martens.be
www.martens.be

Groups visits by arrangement usually focus on the excellent, privately owned Bocholter Brouwerij-museum, which is not usually opened to the general public. Those who use the brewery's conference centre have access too.

For others the brewery tap is the brown and well-used **Bierketel** café, opposite the brewery gates, which opens every day except Thursday, from 10.00.

Mort Subite Oude Gueuze

7% alcohol by volume
Beer style Oude gueuze
37.5 cl bottles only
UK importer Belgian Beer Import (Bierlijn)
US importer Shelton Brothers

IT IS A RARE PLEASURE to be able to list a beer from a global corporation as a genuine and unsponsored entrant in a list of the top 100 of anything, though exactly which conglomerate owns it right now is not 100% clear, as recent owners Scottish Courage were taken over in 2000 by both Heineken and Carlsberg.'.

The De Keersmaeker family brewery in Kobbegem looks to the naked eye like any other small to medium-sized post-war brewhouse, accessed from the sleepy market square of a northern Payottenland village, next to the brewery tap. The signs in French saying 'Sudden Death' refer only to the brands after which it is now named, Mort Subite.

TASTING NOTES

Mort Subite Oude Gueuze is slightly hazy with a golden-orange hue, under a relatively stable, small white head. In the nose are solvent, wet wood, green apples and grapefruit. The taste is tart but any sourness is restricted to lactic acid – making it extremely refreshing. There are some obvious wheat notes and it has an esteric character, suggesting some exotic fruit.
Its mouthfeel is refreshing and spritzy, but with some inevitable acidic throat burn. Fruit acids and esters vie for dominance in the aftertaste, neither winning before the fade-out. Make it your last beer of the session and its flavours will linger on your palate for the next half hour.

VERDICT

This is a beautifully restrained authentic oude gueuze, often sold alongside the filtered and sweetened, lightweight version designed for simpler tastes.

Brewery information See p. 81

🍷 Mort Subite Oude Kriek

5.5% alcohol by volume

er style Oude kriek

🍾 37.5 cl bottles only

mporter Belgian Beer Import (Bierlijn)

mporter Shelton Brothers

JUST AS WE WERE recovering from the fact that new Belgian settlers Scottish Courage had re-launched an oude gueuze, news reached us that they would bring out an oude kriek to stand alongside it. Mort Subite? We nearly did.

With the Heinsberg takeover the only change so far has been greater availability. Promoting these two fine beers would be so much more far-sighted than their big rivals BelleVue, who dominate the lambic alcopops market.

Again, this beer is not to be confused with the simpler, sweeter version called simply **Mort Subite Kriek**.

TASTING NOTES

Mort Subite Oude Kriek has a nearly cyclamen pink head, like whipped cream initially, which falls away to leave rings. The beer itself is a deep and hazy garnet red.

Beyond the cherries and their stones are the aromas of Belgian *speculoos* biscuit and freshly cut parsley. Despite the big fruit welcome it is generally very tart, albeit with a rich flavour of sour cherries, again with some faint background *speculoos*. A jumble of oral sensations with lip-smacking fruit, a good sour bite and full fruit fill the texture.

VERDICT

The efforts of multinational corporations to make craft beers usually amount to little more than the creation of gilded fig leaves – beers with old-fashioned names and strap lines trying to hide the inadequacies of lame beer design. Thus far Mort Subite Oude Kriek is a noble exception to that rule. An old-and-new beer in full pomp. Whoever dared to produce it deserves our grateful thanks for their bravery.

Brouwerij Mort Subite
Lierput 1, 1730 Kobbegem
T 02 454 11 11   **F** 02 452 43 10   www.alkenmaes.be

Brewery visits can be arranged for groups.

For casual visitors the nearest you will get to the brewhouse is the **Wit Paard** café on the village square (3 Lierput), next to the main gate, which opens every day except Tuesday, from 10.30 onwards. This simple local is in its fifth generation of family ownership but is undergoing a slight renaissance since the brewery returned to making some traditional products. Rumours of a draught lambic and *kriekenlambic* have not materialised yet.

Drinking Orval at Moeder Lambic, a small street-corner café in Brussels (St Gilles)

Orval

6.2% alcohol by volume

Beer style | Pale ale

33 cl bottles only

UK importer | James Clay & Sons

US importer | Merchant du Vin

THE ABBEY OF ORVAL was founded in 1132, sacked in 1793 by Napoleon and reconstructed on its original site in 1926. Its setting, in the far southwest of Luxembourg province, is eye-catchingly gorgeous.

The brewery and its beer were created in 1931 to help to pay for the rebuilding of the abbey, assisted by a set of Belgian postage stamps. This unique pale ale is bottle-fermented in part with Brettanomyces, then heavily dry-hopped before bottling.

TASTING NOTES

Served in its typical thick-stemmed chalice, Orval presents a typical orangey colour with the hint of a haze. Served at the right temperature it has a thick, just-off-white head that collapses slowly but remains to the end of the drink. The nose is bitter in a complex way, from vegetables, spices and flowers, though this does not prevent the hops showing a marked presence. The taste starts as complex bitterness but is soon balanced by malt, with hints of sweetness, but without becoming really sweet. At the back of the nose are mandarin zest, hop shoots and olives without any oily feeling. The carbonation is perfect, like naturally carbonated spring water or a milder form of *Champenoise*. It's neither chewy nor watery, and instead of a new aftertaste, the bitterness lingers on.

VERDICT

Its drinkability is second to none. This is the most popular session beer for discerning beer drinkers in Belgium, with something there whatever one's mood. In that sense it is unparalleled.

[TW ADDS: a few years back I was so taken with Orval that I termed it 'God's home-brew'. Sadly in recent years I see it becoming more mainstream, with less bitterness, little obvious Brettanomyces and fewer of the other characteristics that made it great. In my view it needs re-invigorating.]

Brasserie de l'Abbaye Notre-Dame d'Orval SA
Orval 2, 6823 Villers-devant-Orval
T 061 31 12 61   **E** brasserie@orval.be
www.orval.be

It is not possible to visit the brewery though you may visit the ruins of the old, vacated abbey and by arrangement stay as a paying guest on retreat at the current working abbey.

The **Ange Gardien** tavern (3 Rue d'Orval) is a huge refectory-like café a few hundred metres from the abbey gates. It opens from March to November, every day except Monday, from 11.30 to 19.30. In July and August it opens daily from 10.00 to 21.00, serving a wholesome range of simple snacks and the beers and cheeses made at the abbey.

Brother Xavier outside Orval Abbey

Proef

 Reinaert Tripel

9% alcohol by volume

er style: Tripel

33 cl bottles only

mporter Belgian Beer Import (Bierlijn)

mporter Shelton Brothers

THE PROEF BREWERY in Lochristi, between Ghent and Antwerp, is an extraordinary creation. It is a commercial off-shoot from one of the university schools of brewing in Ghent, which is unusual but hardly world-beating. However, in terms of its production values it may well be unique.

The word *proef* can mean 'taste' or 'trial' in Dutch and this brewery, in effect, brews taste trials for its customers.

Dirk Naudts and his team have brewed literally thousands of different beers for hundreds of customers over the years. They will brew beers for anyone. Private customers can order a brew for private consumption or to send their employees at Christmas. 'Wannabe' brewers can get professional opinions on their ideas. And existing commercial breweries can commission experimental 'what if' brews.

For aspiring brewers the existence of Proef is a godsend, enabling them to make good quality beers without having to invest in their own expensive kit. The only downside is that they lose the chance to learn by their own mistakes. For the team here are nothing if not excellent technical brewers.

For their parent company, Andelot, they also make their own range of beers under the Reinaert brand.

TASTING NOTES
Reinaert Tripel is a dark yellow tripel with little UFOs, sporting a huge fluffy snow-white head. The nose has mainly aromatic hops, with a faint cake aroma and the white candy sugar imprint that brewers say one cannot trace. The taste, however, is liquorice-sweet with vegetable and a lesser hoppy bitterness, that does not blend in but clashes with the strange sweetness. It is full-bodied – more so than a drier tripel. There is some dryness all the same, but nowhere near the attenuation one expects from the likes of Westmalle.

VERDICT
We knew we would disagree about this one. JPP reckons this is a workaday industrial tripel among many. For TW this is an excellent example of an honestly crafted strong, amber-blond beer that is unmistakably a tripel rather than a Duvel look-alike or strong blonde. You decide.

Proef brewer Dirk Naudts

BVBA Andelot
Doornzelestraat 20, 9080 Lochristi-Hijfte
T 09 356 71 02   **F** 09 356 71 03
E info@proefbrouwerij.com

The brewery cannot be visited and has no tasting café.

🍷 Vicaris Generaal

8.8% alcohol by volume

Beer style | Strong brown ale

33 cl bottles only

UK importer | Belgian Beer Import (Bierlijn)

US importer | This beer is not exported to the US yet

THERE ARE roughly a hundred different companies in Belgium that present themselves as a 'brewery' but do not own a brewhouse. By far the biggest outlay that a commercial brewer has to make when setting up their business is the cost of the kit and of a building in which to put it. By getting other brewers to make the beers for you, costs go down markedly. Sadly, so does quality control very often.

The Dilewyns family used to operate a brewery many years ago and those inexpert in reading Belgian beer labels and brewery websites can be forgiven for believing that they still do. In fact, they are one of several dozen companies that get Proef to make their beers for them.

That said, do not let any of the above put you off. These guys have created, with the Proef team, an interesting range of beers, of which this is the best in our view. And who knows, the birth of a new brewery may be just around the corner.

TASTING NOTES

Generaal is a dark amber beer, not always sporting a head. It has an unbelievably burnt nose, roasted but great. With just a touch of sweetness, the rest is like a nicely baked fresh bread crust. Are we to suspect Maillard in the cooking vessel? Surely not at the Proef? Burnt, roasted, coffee-like, maybe mocha. It is medium-bodied, and can have low carbonation, though not always.

VERDICT

Vicaris 'Brouwerij' may be a bit naughty by missing one of the key components its business name implies but they clearly put a lot of thought into the conversations they have with their partners the brewers. Theirs are among the best beers from the 'virtual brewers'.

Vicaris Brouwerij
Vijfbunderstraat 31, 9200 Grembergen
T 052 20 18 57   E info@vicaris.be
www.vicaris.be

We have not heard from anyone who has been there but we understand that this not-a-brewery opens its doors to visitors on Wednesday and Saturday afternoons between 14.00 and 18.00.

Beersel Lager

5.5% alcohol by volume

er style Blond lager

33 cl bottles and occasionally on draught

mporter This beer in not exported yet

mporter This beer is not exported yet

THE REASONS WHY commercial brewers use Proef's services vary. Sometimes they want to try out something new on a short run, or test out what would happen if a recipe or brewing method were to change, or as in this case because you do not want to go brewing a lager in a lambic brewery. (And because Armand and Dirk wanted to know what it would taste like if you made a true Bohemian Pilsener with a Belgian hop mix.)

TASTING NOTES

The head on Beersel Lager is gone in seconds, but leaves a transparent rim and layers of textbook lace. This is a pale gold beer with a slight haze. The nose is highly hopped but also grapy, with a lasting biscuit background.

The taste is also highly hoppy, the 'Belgian' hops imparting a slightly metallic character. Beyond these, a honey flavour appears, quite fruity for a lager. One can taste the *Krausening*. Far from being light, as one would expect, it has filling and texture, alongside a serious hop bite.

VERDICT

This rather nice Belgian interpretation of Bohemian Pilsner tastes like it could come from an American micro, despite the old-world hops. And we like the fact it scrupulously avoids the 'Pilsner' moniker, using the more mundane word 'lager'.

Brewery information *See p. 50*

🍷 de Ranke Kriek

7% alcohol by volume
Beer style **Kriekenbier**
75 cl bottles only
UK importer Belgian Beer Import (Bierlijn); & Shelton Brothers UK
US importer Shelton Brothers

NINO BACELLE and GUIDO DEVOS began making
beer in the mid-Nineties, hiring other people's
breweries initially to make some house beers for
the Bierwinkel at Wevelgem, near Kortrijk.
For many years they hired the underused Deca
brewery at Woesten, near Poperinge in the
hop-growing region of West Flanders.

In 2005, they opened their own plant in
Dottignies (1a Rue Petit Tourcoing), near Mouscron,
managing a seamless transition with no fall in
quality and fulfilling a long-standing ambition.
The decision to move the production end of the
operation south of the language border raised
Flemish eyebrows. However, in truth it is much
easier to open a new brewery in Wallonia, the
French-speaking south of Belgium, than in Flanders,
the more fiscally conservative Dutch-speaking
north. And the beer does not seem to mind.

Nowadays they concentrate on making a small
range of beers that are typically Belgian, in that
they are untypical of anything. And like all the
great breweries, they strive perpetually to improve
what they do, combining a great experimental
spirit with the desire to attain consistency.

TASTING NOTES

Under a pinkish head that disappears in four
seconds lurks a deep garnet red, slightly hazy beer
with a brownish tinge. Can a nose be tart? If so,
this one is, offering also aromas of ripened cherries
and cherry must, Cherry Heering and port wine,
though there is nothing of sherry or Madeira here.
On tasting we find again an outspoken tartness,
with an extremely woody character, like old oak.
The acidity is nearly lemon-like, only a small step
away from the best lambic-based kriek. It finishes
with earthy aromas and flavours as from over-ripe
fruit, or pressed grape pulp, in among the cherry.
For an acid-dry fruit beer, it is quite well-bodied,
though the acidity thins this effect, falsely. Your
front teeth will notice the classical dry-out effect.

VERDICT

A great example of what a dry cherry ale can be,
with lambic nuances. A hellishly interesting drink.

Brewery information *See p. 90*

BREWERY de Ranke

Guldenberg

8.5% alcohol by volume

beer style Strong blond ale

33 cl & 75 cl bottles and occasionally on draught

importer Belgian Beer Import (Bierlijn); & Shelton Brothers UK

importer Shelton Brothers

ALTHOUGH YOU CAN now find de Ranke beers as far afield as Tokyo and New York, the brewery's focus has always been delightfully local. Their original tripel was a slightly sweet and spicy brew called **Wevelgemse** which is still found around the town. When they created a bolder, hoppier and altogether more cultured beer, they gave it the name Guldenberg, also the name of the town's centre for performance arts, appropriately.

With the success of **XX Bitter** (p. 90) Guldenberg took the route from sweet and spicy to herbal and hoppy.

TASTING NOTES

Guldenberg pours clear golden, with a generous, whipped-egg-white head that leaves irregular fine lacing. Against an incongruous background of roasted malt comes the aroma of ginger, peppery hop and some nutmeg. The taste surprises, with far more hop than the nose suggested, taking attention away from a firm malt base. In the background is brandy, but with a suggestion that someone slipped Amaretto into the cake too. By the finish, assertive hop bitterness has given way to a sweet and spicy finish.

VERDICT

A refined, high-brow, strong ale that used to make a great 'dessert beer' before it went hoppy but is now good enough to enjoy any time the taste buds need waking.

Brewery information *See p. 90*

🍷 XX Bitter

6.2% alcohol by volume

Beer style | Bitter beer
🍾🛢 **33** cl & **75** cl bottles and occasionally on draught
UK importer | Belgian Beer Import (Bierlijn); & Shelton Brothers UK
US importer | Shelton Brothers

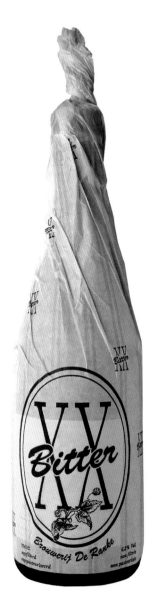

XX BITTER was originally based loosely on **Orval** (p. 84), but as that beer has reduced in its use of hops, so XX Bitter had taken the same path in the opposite direction, spawning a new generation of bitter beers in Flanders, to accompany the revival of saison in the south.

TASTING NOTES

This light golden beer, under a relatively stable but slight, white, head just begs to be tried. The aroma? Hops! Hops!! HOPS!!! The taste is an immediate attack of hop bitters, offset by something roasted, like malted cookies. These roasted notes blend fabulously with the omnipresent hops to make a great balance. Though it is no more than medium-bodied, it has a very quaffable quality, and only a moderate impression of alcohol. In the aftertaste the bitterness keeps going and going.

VERDICT

This was the first, and for some years the only, supremely hoppy beer in Belgium. It has progressed over the years, thus far improving all the time. It is difficult to see how much better it could get. Its character will even survive being served iced on hot summer days.

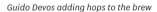

Guido Devos adding hops to the brew

Brouwerij De Ranke
Brugstraat 43, 8560 Wevelgem
T&F 056 41 82 41 **E** info@deranke.be
www.deranke.be

Brewery visits are unlikely, even for groups. The family's beer shop (www.bierwinkel.be) is at 47–49 Roeselarestraat and is open from Monday to Saturday from 09.00 to 12.00 and 13.00 to 18.30, stocking all the brewery's beers including a few made especially for them.

Regenboog

🍷 't Smisje Dubbel

9% alcohol by volume

eer style Dubbel

🍾 🛢 **33** cl bottles and occasionally on draught

importer Belgian Beer Import (Bierlijn)

importer B. United International

BREWER JOHAN BRANDT has been threatening to move his makeshift brewery from the former smithy (*smisje* in old Dutch) in the suburbs of Bruges to a purpose-built small plant near Oudenaarde in East Flanders for at least five years. The plans keep getting delayed by the fact that everyone wants to buy his beers, of which there are over a dozen, brewed on rotation when stocks appear to be low.

This one was formerly known as Dubbel Dadel, as it contains essence of dates (Du: *dadel*).

TASTING NOTES

't Smisje Dubbel is a dark brown beer, with a white head that dissipates slowly. It boasts a fruity nose, with candy and something of sweet fortified wine. The taste is predominantly sweet but with a roasted malt surround. A bitterish kick suggests herbs or cocoa powder, rather than spices or strong hopping. There remains a fruity taste too, plus a flavour that may comes from preserved dates. The balance is quite good. Unsurprisingly, it has a rich mouthfeel, the alcohol being obvious but restrained.

VERDICT

Complex enough to be a winter ale, though it is available all year round. The best of the brewery's regular beers in our opinion.

Brewery information See p. 92

't Smisje Calva Reserva

12% alcohol by volume

Beer style Barley wine

25 cl bottles only

UK importer This beer is not exported to the UK

US importer B. United International

THE EXPORT MARKET is fickle. Some otherwise excellent breweries steer clear of it altogether while others have yet to be invited to dance. Other brewers are courted early in their development and end up sending more beer across the oceans than they supply to their local wholesalers.

Johan Brandt is a most affable giant of a man and Bruges is a popular tourist destination for travelling American beer lovers. So really his brewery's fate was sealed before he began.

At least three of his beers were made initially for his American importer, of which this extraordinary, three-times fermented barley wine, is the most immense. He sometimes takes some stick for creating beers only for the US. Lucky Americans, poor us, we say.

TASTING NOTES

Calva Reserva is an amber-red beer usually found hazy, with a slight bronze sheen under a stable, yellow-amber head that leaves lacing. In the nose, the sherry wood leaps out, bringing with it lactate and a touch of rotting apple. In the taste you find dried fruit – cherries, apples, figs maybe. There is no sweetness, this being off-set by restrained lactate, tannin bitterness and slight spiciness. Can you call something frivolously complex? In the finish, there is something like berries steeped in alcohol. Its impressive body has a robust but slick texture, almost oily, and yes that word complex again.

VERDICT

This is severe beer. A major creation to be kept for special occasions.

Brouwerij de Regenboog
Koningin Astridlaan 134, 8310 Assebroek-Brugge
T 050 37 38 33   **F** 050 37 38 41
E smisje@pandora.be

No brewery visits as such and no brewery tap. This may be the only brewery in the world to be based in a honey shop. This opens from Tuesday to Friday from 09.00 to 12.00 and 14.00 to 19.00, plus Saturday afternoons till 18.00. It sells the beers too.

Rochefort 8°

9.2% alcohol by volume

er style Dubbel

33 cl bottles only

mporter Beer Direct & James Clay & Sons

mporter Merchant du Vin

THE ABBEY OF ST. RÉMY was founded originally as a nunnery in 1230 but became a Cistercian monastery in 1464. There was a brewery here from the late 16th century until the French revolution did away with the abbeys in 1794.

The monks who came to reclaim St. Rémy in 1887 were assisted by brothers from the cloisters at Achel to create a small-scale brewery in 1899, a favour returned with good grace exactly a century later, when Père Antoine from St. Rémy assisted with the creation of the brewery at Achel (p. 17).

The brewers of Rochefort are unique among the Trappist abbeys in keeping all their beers dark. Each of the monks resident at the abbey is allowed one bottle of beer each day, though in practice none takes up the option except on special occasions and festivals.

TASTING NOTES

Rochefort 8 is murky brown – appearance is not its strong point. Its dense, yellowish head collapses with full lacing. The nose has bananas, plums and pears, plus some roasted malts and what some Belgians call 'students' oats' – a mix of hazelnuts, walnuts, almonds and raisins. Its taste includes bitter pears. The velvety texture is powered by an underbuild of malts, both roasted and pale. There is a charming retronasal aroma of almonds. The alcohol is brandy-like and there are higher alcohols there too, whilst the mouthfeel is thick and nourishing.

VERDICT

In the past, monks' beer was called 'liquid bread'. In that context, this is a wholemeal brown loaf straight from the oven. Impressive, is the word that springs to mind.

Brewery information *See p. 94*

Rochefort

Rochefort 10°

11.3% alcohol by volume

Beer style: Strong abbey-style ale

33 cl and occasionally **75** cl bottles

UK importer Beer Direct & James Clay & Sons

US importer Merchant du Vin

ROCHEFORT 10, or *noir* as it is sometimes known, is the newest of the abbey's beers but perhaps the most memorable. As with the other beers it is made with the faintest dab of coriander. It uses spicing to draw out and enhance the flavour of the beer, rather than murder it.

TASTING NOTES

10 is a deep, dark brown beer with a reddish hue, and a dense, stable, creamy head that laces nicely. The smell of banana, chocolate, toffee, ripe pear and hops hints at what is to come. What to say about its taste? It is almost too rich, not purely in flavour but also in mouthfeel, which is nearly chewy. There is chocolate, double cream, vintage port, Madeira, raisins and aromatic wood, enlivened by sweetness and a bitter-peppery root spice – maybe horseradish or daikon. Alcohol features. There is tartness somewhere too, mainly in the aftertaste, which features *crème de noix* on a bed of velvety roasted malt. Ageing in the cellar produces liquorice sweetness, along with something of a dark aperitif wine, such as *Pineau des Charentes*. The older beer is richer, as the esters and oxidation attack that chewiness.

VERDICT

Is there a better beer to store in a cellar for a decade or two? The ultimate beer for contemplation.

Brasserie de Rochefort
Abbaye Notre Dame de St. Rémy
Rue de l'Abbaye 8, 5580 Rochefort
T 084 21 31 81   **F** 084 22 10 75
E saint.remy@belgacom.net
www.trappistes-rochefort.com

The abbey allows people to attend some of its religious services by arrangement, and with due deference. Otherwise visits are a rare event.
    Rochefort is the only Trappist brewery not to have an official tasting café. The nearest equivalent is the convivial and quietly accomplished **Relais de Saint Rémy** (140 Route de Ciney), some two kilometres further out of town on the road that passes the abbey. It is closed on Wednesdays and from 14.30 on Tuesdays but otherwise opens daily from 10.00 to 21.30. Perfectly kept beers and reliable cooking.

Rodenbach (Palm)

Oud Belegen Foederbier

6% alcohol by volume

er style Aged brown ale

25 cl, 33 cl & occasionally 75 cl bottles

nporter This beer is never exported

nporter This beer is never exported

THE RODENBACHS were to 19th century Flanders much as the Mitford sisters were to 20th century England. They got everywhere, from featuring in the political development of a nation to crafting great works, though in this case it was beer rather than novels.

Their St. George's brewery is extraordinary for its great temple halls of massive oak tuns (Du: *foeders*; Fr: *foudres*), in which the building blocks of all their beers, oak-aged brown ales aged for eighteen months to two years, are grown. The actual brewing has, since 2001, been based in a brewhouse that would not be out of place in Huxley's *Brave New World*. It is the fermentation that comes from the Middle Ages.

Foederbier is the building block from which the remarkable Rodenbach beers are made.

TASTING NOTES

Foederbier can sport a huge, dense yellow head over a hazy amber beer, though this sometimes collapses swiftly, which we take to be a reflection of the fact that every tun is different. The pungent lactic acid nose can have true wine characteristics, going as far as replicating specific grapes, depending on the tun in question. In some bottles there is no discernable acetic acid, which is interesting. Usually it leaves soft, woody, lactic, yoghurt-like flavours, whilst some residual sugar is apparent. There are also strawberry, cherry wood and milk chocolate. It is said that sparklers on the handpulls smoothen the flavours. There is some acid burn at least, yet it remains medium bodied. In the aftertaste, there is more oak.

VERDICT

This rare beer clearly varies depending on the vat from which it is drawn. Giving it a try is an essential stepping stone on the way to understanding oak-aged ales done the Flemish way. Warn your salivary glands first though.

Brewery information *See p. 96*

Rodenbach (Palm)

Rodenbach Grand Cru

6% alcohol by volume

Beer style Aged brown ale

 25 cl, **33** cl & occasionally **75** cl bottles, and on draught

UK importer James Clay & Sons

US importer Duvel Moortgat USA

TO MAKE GRAND CRU, the contents of several tuns are blended and the beer is sweetened slightly with glucose, which the longstanding brewer Rudi Ghequire says has happened since before he arrived at the brewery in the early 1980s. To keep the pH just the right side of meltdown into intolerable acidity, it is then filtered so finely that it may as well have been pasteurised.

The plan to replace the old brewhouse at Rodenbach was hatched soon after the takeover by the Palm brewery group in 1998. 'As any fule do knoe', all brewery takeovers mark the beginning of a downward spiral to oblivion. So when the old Rodenbach sharpness disappeared for a time the worst was feared. In practice, the change occurred in response to a simple question. Is acetic acid (i.e. vinegar) ever a legitimate component of beer? The overlords at Palm and a lot of sensitive beer drinkers said 'no'. So Palm removed most of it by cleaning out and shoring up the tuns, thus reducing the oxidation that occurred within them.

And when they had done so, a big row broke out about why the beer had gone downhill.

In fact it is that very dab of acetic acid that marks out Grand Cru as the beer of near-crazed genius that it is. That and the fact that their chief creator, Rudi Ghequire, claims never to have produced a beer he considers perfect.

TASTING NOTES

The ultimate oud bruin has a blackcurrant or burgundy sheen; protected by a yellowish-brown head, that is dense (despite its acidity) and lacy. An immediately recognisable woody nose, with lactic acid, and a touch of black cherry is vinous. The taste is vinous too, with sharp notes both of lactic and acetic acid. Yet there is some sweetness under all the tangle of sour tastes, from a small amount of sugar added late in fermentation. Overall, this beer is astringent, with a dental dry-out effect sparked by a low pH. A multitude of esters do not prevent it having a remarkably clean palate. At the finish a twist of metallic oxide comes in from somewhere. The late Michael Jackson knew what he was saying when he described this as the most refreshing beer in the world.

VERDICT

This is a masterpiece on a spectrum of excellence that encompasses the oak-aged oud bruin beers of Verhaege (p. 125) and others too. An absolute must on any beer lover's tour of the world of beer. If this beer does not stop you in your tracks and make you question all you knew thus far, you may need a taste bud transplant.

NV Brouwerij Rodenbach
Spanjestraat 133–141, 8800 Roeselare
T 051 22 34 00   **F** 051 22 92 48
E webmaster@rodenbach.be
www.rodenbach.be

Group visits by prior arrangement are easy to arrange on Monday to Thursday via the website. If a tour is already running that day they are happy to tag on extra visitors by prior arrangement (**T** 051 27 28 10).

In addition the brewery hosts conferences, meals for 20 or more people, banquets and weddings receptions by arrangement. And boy is this a great place for a wedding reception.

On the market square in the centre of town, the incongruously modern **Zalm** café (24 Grote Markt) is one of the few bars in which Foederbier can be sampled – though expect a look that says, "Travelling beer nut, then?" It opens every day except Wednesday, from 09.00 (11.00 Sundays), closing early on Tuesdays and Sundays.

Brewer Rudi Ghequire

La Rulles Estivale

5.2% alcohol by volume

er style Bitter beer

75 cl bottles and occasionally on draught

nporter Belgian Beer Import (Bierlijn)

nporter B. United International

WHEN GRÉGORY VERHELST started brewing commercially in 1998, in the Gaume region of southern Luxembourg, he was determined to do two things. He would produce only a single blonde ale but get good at it, and he would always sell most of his beer in the Pays Gaumaise.

Thankfully he has broken both promises. His range of beers has expanded and you can find his beers from Baltimore to Brussels, though he still sells more within twenty kilometres of his home village than anywhere else.

This will not last. If he stays true to his standards, the world will beat a path to his door.

TASTING NOTES

With Estivale we find a hazy golden beer filling our glass, sparkling with an orange sheen, well carbonated and with a whipped cream head that is comfortingly irregular. In a phenomenal combination of aromas, a superbly fine hop nose strikes first, followed by *honingbollen* (a honey-flavoured sweet for Dutch and Flemish children) and nectar-laden blossoms. There is honey again in the taste, fulfilling the promise of the name, *Estivale* meaning mid-summer. The finish is however very much hop-bitter with a touch of citrus, though the balance is just about perfect.

VERDICT

A superb, light, session beer. A Gaumaise take on the rebirth of saison, perhaps.

Brewery information *See p. 98*

La Rulles Triple

8.4% alcohol by volume

Beer style Tripel

75 cl bottles and occasionally on draught

UK importer Belgian Beer Import (Bierlijn)

US importer B. United International

GRÉGORY'S FIRST BEER WAS **La Rulles Blonde**, which did indeed take several years to perfect. His second, a brune, was initially a disaster, but improved quite quickly. This tripel was his third and was born fully formed.

TASTING NOTES

This is a peach-coloured ale, sporting an ochre head that reduces fast to a half centimetre. Its nose has both herbal and spicy aromas – like ginger with laurel and garden weeds. Its remarkable taste is somehow medicinal, with flavours of mint, camphor and wood stain. But don't panic, these are nuances not dominant traits – the overall effect is mild and makes for interesting drinking. The main character is more typically tripel. Candy, some yeastiness and at the finish just a touch of citrus. Fuller bodied than many.

VERDICT

Being well-bodied puts it some way off a mainstream tripel but its classiness marks it out as a legitimate and interesting variant rather than a failed imitation.

Brasserie Artisanale de Rulles SPRL
Rue Maurice Grévisse 36, 6724 Rulles-Habay
T 063 41 18 38   **F** 063 41 18 55
E info@larulles.be
www.larulles.be

Group visits by arrangement only.
The nearest thing they have to a brewery tap is the **Buffet de la Gare** at Marbehan train station, a country stop on the main line between Brussels and Luxembourg. This marvellous institution opens every day except Wednesday, from 10.00 onwards, though it closes at 15.00 on Sundays.

🍷 St. Feuillien Triple

8.5% alcohol by volume

er style   Tripel

🍾   **150** cl, **300** cl, **450** cl, **600** cl and occasionally even **900** cl (!) bottles

mporter   Beer Direct

mporter   Artisanal Imports

FIVE GENERATIONS of the Friart family have run a brewery on this site. It was closed between 1977 and 1988, during which time they developed a drinks business, named St. Feuillien after its main brands.

Most St. Feuillien brand beers are actually made by the Brasserie du Bocq in their nice-looking but production line brewery in the Meuse Valley. These are nowhere near as nice as the ones made at the old family brewery, which are distinguished generally by appearing in unfeasibly large bottles, often under exactly the same name.

There are clearly tensions here that need to be resolved. You cannot have a single brand coming in two palpably different forms, one for the international market in good taste and the other for the cash and carry.

In 2005, all St. Feuillien Triple was made at the family's own brewery. In 2007 we tasted, in successive weeks, a 150 cl bottle of amber nectar and a 75 cl bottle of badly perfumed frippery, both labelled St. Feuillien Triple. Ho hum.

TASTING NOTES

This is an orange-gold beer with a fine, dense yellow head that is stable and fed by good pearling. The nose is peppery-spicy with citrus overtones and betrays candy sugar, as well as a slightly sour touch. A sweet, young malt taste conquers over all, with a retronasal bouquet of honey and spices – coriander, Curaçao orange peel and what? Unmistakably well attenuated, more so when cellar-aged, the texture that begins with slick malt ends on alcohol! Yet there is also a residual sweetness, apparent in the aftertaste.

VERDICT

Until the branding confusion ends, the best way to sort the wheat from the chaff is to stick to the large bottles – 150 cl and above. A case of size appearing to matter.

Brasserie Saint-Feuillien
Rue d'Houdeng 20, 7070 Le Roeulx
T 064 64 18 18
E info@st-feuillien.com
www.st-feuillien.com

Group tours by arrangement only.

Stouterik

4.5% alcohol by volume

Beer style: Stout

33 cl bottles and occasionally on draught

UK importer: Belgian Beer Import (Bierlijn); & Shelton Brothers UK

US importer: Shelton Brothers

THE SENNE is the river that runs beneath Brussels after dribbling its way through Payottenland. The equivalent operation in Scandinavia – Nøgne Ø – uses the strap line 'The Uncompromising Brewery', and the same spirit applies here.

The thing that drives Bernard Leboucq and Yvan De Baets is indignation with the sloppy way in which so many small Belgian breweries try to mimic the efforts of large industrial breweries by producing technically perfect, dreary imitations of fundamentally bland products.

If there is such a thing as justice, then these two will both become rich men – though they will hate that. Already they make three of the best beers in Belgium and this is before they have a brewery. Bernard used to have one, St. Pieters at Sint-Pieters-Leeuw in Payottenland, which closed in 2006 when he outgrew it.

They are working on a replacement and with luck will have one by 2009, somewhere in the city's environs. For now they hire the brewhouse at de Ranke, where Yvan trained.

Their two other beers, a hybrid of ale and lambic called **Crianza**, and **Equinox**, the winter ale would both have been considered for these pages too, had the intention not been to develop them further.

TASTING NOTES

Stouterik is a fully black beer. Its fluffy, medium cream-brown head given a pinkish sheen that goes down leaving some lace. There is some pine in the aroma, with parsley, cypress, tobacco, wood stain, roasted malts and hops. The taste confirms the swirl of aromas, yielding ink, American hops, dried black mushrooms and some more peppery flavours. There is some undeniable sweetness but it is kept in check perfectly by all those dark, roasted influences. At the back of the nose is a little cigar ash. Not very big bodied, but nowhere near thin either. The tobacco flavour flows on for quite a long time.

VERDICT

There is no doubting that in global terms this is a really great stout and an exciting beer. Lacking the scorched barley taste of a classical Irish stout – though who said it was trying to be Irish? This may be the first really original Belgian stout.

Brewery information *See p. 102*

🍷 Taras Boulba

4.5% alcohol by volume
beer style Light ale
33 cl bottles and on draught
importer Belgian Beer Import (Bierlijn); & Shelton Brothers UK
importer Shelton Brothers

TARAS BOULBA was the epononymous hero of the novel by Gogol, in which a semi-retired colonel is moved to foul deeds in the name of nationalism, when his sons return from their studies at university to the Ukraine.

You have to name a beer after something.

TASTING NOTES

Taras Boulba is a fully hazy-yellow beer, displaying a little greenish sheen under a slowly receding, off-white head. The nose yields aromas of parsley, grass, grain, and a bit of chaff. This is a beer that really tastes of beer – grainy in general, malty in particular and with necessary touches of sweetness, confident bitterness and a dryish ending. Chaff too, as expected this in this summery kind of beer. Dry in the bottle, less so on draught.

VERDICT

JPP rates this as a good summer brew, while TW goes a lot further.

[TW ADDS: Taras Boulba is in my Belgian top ten and I try to keep some it in my cellar at all times to impress guests that Belgium can produce light beers of greatness too.]

Yvan De Baets and Bernard Leboucq interview for their new marketing manager

Brewery information *See p. 102*

Senne (at de Ranke)

Zinnebir

6% alcohol by volume

Beer style Bitter beer

33 cl & **75** cl bottles, and on draught

UK importer Belgian Beer Import (Bierlijn); & Shelton Brothers UK

US importer Shelton Brothers

ZINNEBIR was Bernard Leboucq's original beer at St. Pieters. Since those early days it has transformed from a workmanlike, honest pale ale into a beautifully crafted beer of great confidence.

TASTING NOTES

Zinnebir is an amber-orange, crystal clear ale with yeast that sediments out impressively. Its head is stable and off-white. It has a nose reminiscent of the malt and hops smell that greets the first visitors to a well-presented beer festival. Faint citrus peel can be detected too. It has always had a slightly strange, but not unpleasant sweaty, bitter taste. This has receded, with recent versions absorbing it into a more hop-bitter character. Some amber malt is obvious, and a slight spicy touch. It is not dense but rather is dry, suggesting high attenuation.

VERDICT

For a relatively new brewery this is a technically impressive beer that clearly gets better with the passage of time. A modern classic in the making.

Brasserie de la Senne
T 0497 93 23 75
www.brasseriedelasenne.be

As it does not exist yet, the brewery cannot be visited.

If you want to find the spirit of the future brewery on display visit Bruxellensis, the cutest and best informed beer festival on Belgian soil, held each year in some garage in the incidental backstreets of inner Brussels, the coolest and dampest political hotbed in the world.
See www.festivalbruxellensis.be.

Senne beers at the Bruxellensis beer festival

Grottenbier Bruin

6.5% alcohol by volume

beer style Dubbel

33 cl & **75** cl bottles

importer James Clay & Sons; & Belgian Beer Import

importer Artisanal Imports

EVARIST DECONINCK was a cheese maker before he became a brewer. He started making cheese for the French monks of the Refuge of Saint Bernard from 1934 until 1959. Before long he was also in collaboration with the Abbey of Sint Sixtus in Westvleteren, for whom he brewed beer in the hop lands of West Flanders.

The purpose of his brewery was to produce and distribute a range of beers called 'St. Sixtus' that were licensed imitations of the abbey's own beers, in order that those beers had some representation in the wider world. However, the fact these were imitations meant they were never taken into the hearts of beer lovers and in 1992 the Order ended the licence. By rights the brewery should have folded but this was not in its owner's nature.

The brand was changed to Sint-Bernardus. Then they produced a blond beer for the first time. The rest of the range was improved and in a few years this most utilitarian of breweries was one of the best in Belgium. Its success is built on the fact that most of its ales are fermented gently, over a longer period than most others.

Accolades followed, with none more prestigious that the fact that Pierre Celis, the man behind the revival of white beers in Belgium and beyond, chose the Saint Bernard brewery (its correct name) to be his preferred partner in the production of a new brown beers called *Grottenbier*, named as such because, initially at least, they were matured in caves (Du: *grotten*) at Kanne, near Maastricht.

TASTING NOTES

Grottenbier is a muddy, dark brown ale with a medium, tan-cream head that is more stable when the beer is young. The nose includes grapes and old wine, enriched with nutty and flowery aromas. When younger, the beer is fruity and yeasty but with a clear presence of darker malts. In the taste there is rosewater, bitterish cardboard, wood, sweetness and, if aged, tartness at the same time. There is biscuit too, with dark cake and again roasted malts. The texture can be thin, though the younger beer is well bodied and slick.

VERDICT

This is not as complex as most St. Bernardus beers, which suggests fermentation may have been a bit faster. However, it is still offers more than most brown beers of this strength and ages quite well.

Brewery information *See p. 108*

Brewery information *See p. 108*

Sint-Bernardus' huge copper kettles (see p.108)

St. Bernardus Abt 12

10.5% alcohol by volume

Beer style Strong abbey-style ale

33 cl & **75** cl bottles and occasionally on draught

UK importer James Clay & Sons; & Belgian Beer Import

US importer D&V International

IN THE DAYS when Sint-Bernardus was 'St. Sixtus', Abt 12 was the beer based on **Westvleteren 12**, the abbey's fearsome barley wine (see p. 131). As the years pass it continues to grow apart, now developing a following in its own right. The mash contains a remarkably high proportion of candy sugar. Despite this, quality is maintained, probably because of the prolonged fermentation period.

TASTING NOTES

Abt 12 is a deep, dark brown beer, reflecting a reddish sheen. On top grows a thick brown head that retreats with shards of lace. As to the nose, think flambéed banana, rum baba or Viennese *Sachertorte*, plus chocolate and a skid mark of rubber. The taste is sweet, with flavours of liquorice, sweet Belgian chocolate, overripe banana and plum pudding. Some people get figs – if fresh and sweet maybe. The mouthfeel is very heavy, almost chewy. There is also an impression of walnut oil. The flavours keep going all the way through, though there is no new aftertaste except, fleetingly, cigar ash.

VERDICT

A phoenix, risen from the ashes to become a Belgian classic.

Brewery information *See p. 108*

St. Bernardus Tripel

7.5% alcohol by volume

er style   Tripel

🛢   **33** cl & **75** cl bottles and occasionally on draught

mporter   James Clay & Sons; & Belgian Beer Import

mporter   D&V International

THE CREATION of this beer in 1994 marked the point at which the Belgian brewing world realised that the St. Bernard brewery was going for survival. Somewhere in the recesses of an ageing memory we recall its brewer remarking to an eminent beer writer that the loss of the contract that had constituted the brewery's raison d'etre was not an insurmountable problem as "we brew good beer".

When this tripel arrived, its excellence was recognised immediately and it was 'game on'. The rest of the challenge took a decade to overcome but, hey, they are still standing.

TASTING NOTES
Straw-orangey by colour, Sint-Bernardus Tripel sports a thick creamy head. In the nose, special malts abound, along with prominent yeast and touches of coriander and blue cheese. Its taste is bitter, spicy with coriander and, under a pretty complex aroma, very obvious sweetness. For a tripel there is a rich mouthfeel, with obvious alcohol, though not really outspoken.

VERDICT
This is an assuredly sweet tripel, not in the classic style.

*[JPP NOTES: the brewery makes a slightly lighter beer, **Watou Tripel** (7% abv), which can be easier to source and is also recommended.]*

Brewery information   See p. 108

107

St. Bernardus Witbier

5.5% alcohol by volume

Beer style Wheat beer

33 cl bottles and on draught

UK importer James Clay & Sons; & Belgian Beer Import

US importer D&V International

PEOPLE SEARCHING for the original Belgian white beer often turn to **Hoegaarden**, nowadays made, hesitantly at times, by InBev, the locals' world brewer. It appears named after the town that led the white beer revival, though in truth it was a man and not a town that caused it to become popular once more.

If it is authenticity you are looking for, change track and try this West Flanders brew instead, made with informal assistance from Pierre Celis, the man in question and the godfather of *Oud Hoegaards*.

TASTING NOTES

Sint-Bernardus Witbier is a dark, hazy orange beer, with a slight white head. The nose immediately conjures up oranges, dried peel, pepper and coriander. The taste has the classical Curaçao orange flavour, plus a spiciness built on a slightly sweet and sour base. Despite a rather clingy mouthfeel, it has just enough dryness to give it great credibility.

VERDICT

If this were a painting by Magritte, it might be called 'This is not a white beer'.

Brouwerij St. Bernard
Trappistenweg 23, 8978 Watou
T 057 38 80 21   **F** 057 38 80 71
E info@sintbernardus.be
www.sintbernardus.be

Currently, the only way to see the brewery is on a pre-booked group visit.

However, the **Brouwershuys** (**T** 057 38 88 60, **F** 057 38 80 71), an exquisitely charming guesthouse next to the brewery that was the home of a former brewer is under refurbishment and will soon re-open, along with a brewery tasting room open to all.

 Potteloereke

8% alcohol by volume

er style Strong brown ale

33 cl bottles and on draught

nporter Belgian Beer Import

nporter The beers of the Sint Canarus brewery are not exported to the US yet

A LOT OF THE OWNERS of Belgian new wave micro-breweries began life as brewers in larger concerns. So it was for Piet Meirhaeghe, who was brewing at the old Riva brewery in Dentergem when he first set up his weekend hobby brewery in 2003.

The original was in his shed. Production ceased after a year while a purpose-built boutique brewhouse was installed. 2005 saw the arrival of 200-litre brew runs. In due course this will expand to 800 litres a time.

TASTING NOTES

Potteloerke is a dark brown ale with the slightest of hazes, bearing a dark creamy head that disappears slowly. The nose is slightly herbal but is dominated by roasted chocolate malt. The taste is way more surprising. Flavours from pear drops, and roasted and sweet malts come in abundance, there is some vinous character and the special *speculoos* flavour. More so, it is very well bodied without being really heavy, and harbours a slight oily mouthfeel. The alcohol hovers without really striking.

VERDICT

Is this what **Rochefort 7** would taste like?

Huisbrouwerij Sint Canarus
Polderweg 2, 9800 Gottem-Deinze
T&F 051 63 69 31   **E** info@sintcanarus.be
www.sintcanarus.be

The brewery opens its doors on Sundays between 10.00 and 20.00 for casual visitors and group 'tours' – though the walk is not long. They kind of expect you to buy beer to take away. Those served in the tasting room may come with an unusual take on dry hopping.

Slaghmuylder's Kerstbier

5.2% alcohol by volume

Beer style Blond lager

33 cl bottles and on draught

UK importer This beer is not exported yet

US importer This beer is not exported yet

AT SLAGHMUYLDER, the brouwmeester Karel Goddeau rarely produces an uninteresting beer. The brewery's other seasonal lager for Easter time, **Slaghmuylder**'s **Paasbier** could equally have made it to this book, as could the much improved pale ale, **Greut Lauwauitj** and the longer-standing **Witkap Tripel**.

The Slaghmuylder family influence, present since 1860, is undergoing change and with luck and good judgement the company will become more confident and outward looking, without ruining their timeless dedication to quality.

The Witkap brands were taken on in 1979 from the Drie Linden brewery of Brasschaat, near Antwerp. Its former owner, Henrik Verlinden, had been a brewer at Westmalle abbey and was allowed for a time to call these beers 'Trappist' in the days before religious connotation took the copyright route.

TASTING NOTES

Slaghmuylder's Kerstbier (or Christmas Beer) offers a nice, fresh nose of European hops. It is reasonable to assume they must have been used in serious amounts. In the taste, a short shock of hops is followed by sweet pale malts, eventually acquiring a grapey taste. It feels like it should be dry but never quite gets there. The draught, fresh version lends a fresh and hoppy overtone. Like a regular lager dressed in its finest Sunday suit.

VERDICT

There are remarkably few really good lagers brewed in Belgium. The market is dominated by a few rather dull ones that cost a lot less to make. This one, and its stable mate the slightly stronger Paasbier (or Easter Beer) show Belgians what a good quality lager can be like.

Brewery information See p. 111

BREWERY

Slaghmuylder

Witkap Stimulo (US name: Witkap Singel)

6% alcohol by volume

er style Blonde ale

33 cl bottles and on draught

mporter James Clay & Sons

Importer Vanberg & DeWulf

TASTING NOTES

Witkap Stimulo is a pale yellow beer. Its thick-set white head collapses almost immediately. Its character is hard to describe. The fresh, herbal, grassy, hoppy nose is inviting. The taste is much sharper, spicy in some aspects, hinting at possibly mustard seed? Pepper even? In the end though, the yeast grants exotic fruity notes, like papaya or prickly pear. It is well-bodied for such a light beer.

VERDICT

We do not know the technical reasons why Stimulo manages to be different from all the other Belgian blond ales on the market but it is. A beautiful beer, made traditionally with added sparkle.

Brouwerij Slaghmuylder
Denderhoutembaan 2, 9400 Ninove
T 054 33 18 31   **F** 054 33 84 45
E info@witkap.be
www.witkap.be

At the time of writing the only way to see this much-loved family brewery is in a pre-booked group tour, or else at the open day on the second Saturday of August. Hopefully this will change soon, as the brewery is home to a lovely small museum of brewing history that should be better known.

Otherwise all we can say is that Slaghmuylder beers always taste even better in their home town of Ninove, just beyond Payottenland, west of Brussels. Don't ask why – we don't know. But it is true.

Oud Kriekenbier Crombé

5.7% alcohol by volume

Beer style Kriekenbier

33 cl bottles only

UK importer Belgian Beer Import

US importer This beer is not exported to the US yet

MARC STRUBBE's extended family has had a brewery on the family farm for six generations, since 1830, making it as old as Belgium itself. In the tradition of a farming business, his brewery does a little bit of this and a little bit of that. Some well and some... well?

The Crombé family on the other hand could trace its brewery lineage in Zottegem, East Flanders, back ten generations into the late 18th century, before it had to close silently in 2002. Maybe it is this seniority that means the Crombé beers taken on by Strubbe are treated with reverence and sit among the brewery's most reliably entertaining beers. The sediment, or 'Hergist' version of **Oud Zottegems** is worth trying too.

Before the demise of their brewery, Oud Kriekenbier was the finest, best loved and wackiest of the Crombé beers. Cherries were steeped in aged pale ale to make a beer that was dry as a bone, unmistakably cherried and a glorious colour. It also sported a bottle label, retained to this day, that is straight from the era of Monsieur Hulot's Holiday.

TASTING NOTES

The colour of this beer is somewhere between russet and terracotta, nestling under an ochre-pink head that dwindles fast to a rim of a few millimetres. Its dry and sourish cherry nose, with stones, intensifies slowly and in so doing acquires more sweet fruit jam aroma. It is slightly liqueur-like, as if made with ripe red fruit. The taste features dryness at the same time as soft-sweet fruit, more stones and some raspberry and strawberry flavours. Hay notes are present too, in a finish that is sherried. This is some confused beer. The mouthfeel is slick, even a bit oily, though it is medium bodied at best.

VERDICT

The original Crombé Oude Kriek was lagered for up to four years (!) and remains unsurpassed. Any brewer trying to recreate it using modern methods deserves both pity and admiration. Early attempts were embarrassing, and it still wilts a bit, but progress is very much in the right direction.

Brouwerij Strubbe
Markt 1, 8480 Ichtegem
T 051 58 81 16   **F** 051 58 24 46
E info@brouwerij-strubbe.be
www.brouwerij-strubbe.be

Group visits by arrangement only.

Struise Brouwers (at Deca)

REWERY

Aardmonnik

8% alcohol by volume

er style Aged brown ale

33 cl & **75** cl bottles

mporter The beers from Struise Brouwers are not imported to the UK yet

mporter Shelton Brothers

THE STRUISE BROUWERS, or 'Sturdy Brewers' began by making lighter beers such as wheat beer, an 'English' pale ale and a blond, all of which sold reasonably and were barely noticed.

Then they started making short-run, authentic, strong, old ales that taste like they have been steeped as long as an original vat of Worcestershire Sauce. From bit part players cashing in on the beer firm scene, they rose to be seen as the great revivalists, recreating a genre of heavy, aged beers straight from the merchants' ale houses of old Flemish woodcuts.

[TW NOTES: Those of us who thought they might be flogging off some old 'stock ale' found fermenting in the recesses of the Deca warehouse recall being put sharply in our place.]

They are a most interesting bunch. They brewed at Caulier in northern Hainaut to begin with but moved to Deca soon after de Ranke (p. 90) had moved out. They recently invested in new fermenting vessels so as to be able to make larger quantities. We hope when the full vision is delivered it will be something really special. This is still early days.

TASTING NOTES

The head can vary from a good yellowish foam to zilch, while the beer is near black with hints of red-brown. The nice lactic acid nose has earthy aromas and a drape of dry chocolate powder – cocoa made from top quality beans, without any sweetness. Some bottles have a nice woody aroma, enhanced by something that suggests sweet pepper coulis. It is slightly too seriously vinous. The taste is sweeter with fruity hints, but is held in check by some acids, mainly lactic, and by another punch of cocoa. The earthy and leafy embellishments integrate perfectly. There is red wine and blue cheese at the back of the nose.

VERDICT

Struise Brouwers is 'one to watch'. This beer is a resurrection of an ancient type of cask-aged oud bruin that many thought had gone forever. They make 5,000 bottles every two years. The first version missed out on refermentation in the bottle and was flat as a *pannekoek*. The second was considerably livelier and *Champenoise* in character.

VDACO bvba
Landbouwersstraat 18, 8660 De Panne
T 058 28 80 02   **E** info@struisebrouwers.be
www.struisebrouwers.be

These guys hire the Deca brewery from time to time but do not perform in public.

Abbaye de Val-Dieu Grand Cru

10% alcohol by volume

Beer style Strong abbey-style ale

 33 cl & **75** cl bottles and occasionally on draught

UK importer Beer Direct

US importer D&V International

SOMEBODY HAD BEEN commissioning beers called Abbaye de Val-Dieu for years before Benoît Humblet and Alain Pinckaers set up their brewhouse on the old abbey's farm in northern Liège in 1997.

Belgians of whatever persuasion go dewy eyed when the words abbey and beer are mentioned in the same concept but the emphasis here has always been on competence rather than panache, though with a new female brewing engineer, things may change.

TASTING NOTES

Sporting a dense off-white head like a *Bavarois*, Val-Dieu Grand Cru presents as an opaque, dark brown beer with an orange sheen. Its nose is mainly earthy, leafy, mossy, but strangely not enough, all subdued by the inevitable dark malts – this is a Wallonian beer after all. The taste is a mix of cookies and spices, though these can clash, causing a continuous confusion of flavours, mainly sweet, spicy, bitter, and pine essence. It has a slick texture, chewy to just plain fat, with a sweet, liquorice aftertaste.

VERDICT

We agree that this is a good winter ale – not too spicy, though perhaps a tad too sweet. It should improve with ageing. JPP finds it short on character and balance. TW has been impressed at its ability to shine through, even at the end of a long evening.

Brasserie de l'Abbaye du Val-Dieu
Val-Dieu 225, 4880 Aubel
T 087 68 75 85   **F** 087 68 79 58
E info@val-dieu.com
www.val-dieu.com

Excellent group visits are easy to arrange via the website. Lone travellers who roll up when one is due to depart may be shown mercy and allowed to join.

The abbey can be visited in its own right and the **Casse-Croûte** restaurant, which is on site, opens daily with all the brewery's beers on the menu.

Van Den Bossche

 ## Buffalo

6.5% alcohol by volume

beer style Stout

25 cl & **75** cl bottle and on draught

importer Belgian Beer Import

importer This beer is not imported to the US, though D&V International
commissions a 9% abv custom-made version

THE VAN DEN BOSSCHE family have run this small
family-owned brewery since 1897, specialising
historically in brown ales and more recently in its
Pater Lieven brands and Lamoral.

Buffalo was supposedly first brewed for a
village hooley in 1907, when the original Buffalo
Bill's travelling circus played in Sint-Lievens-
Esse's diminutive town square, next to the
brewery. The recipe is said to have survived
unchanged for a century, though it has drifted
from being the brewery staple to an also-ran
product. In recent years it has fared better
though the authenticity waivers a little.

TASTING NOTES

Buffalo is a very dark beer with a brownish-yellow
head that laces the glass. It has little more in the
nose than a touch of brown sugar and a vague
coffee aroma. The taste, however, is much more
outspoken and quite woody in character. There is
mild lactate and a bit of yeast presence that
superimposes itself on the malty underbuild.
It is roasted rather than burnt. Although a
relatively low strength beer and hence light-
bodied, its generous malt content prevents it
from being watery.

VERDICT

We agree that it is the originality of this beer
rather than its excellence that makes it so
attractive. The bottled version is denser and,
on the whole, better. It is half-way between a
Flemish oud bruin and something else.
JPP says top-fermenting Munich Dunkles, while
TW prefers a Flemish take on sweet stout.

Brouwerij Van Den Bossche
St. Lievensplein 16, 9550 Sint-Lievens-Esse
T 054 50 04 11   **F** 054 50 04 06
E info@paterlieven.be
www.paterlieven.be

Group visits by arrangement only.

Belgian hop trellises in winter

🍷 Kapittel Abt

10% alcohol by volume

Beer style   Strong abbey-style ale

   33 cl & **75** cl bottles

UK importer   James Clay & Sons; & Belgian Beer Import

US importer   Global Beer Network

FOUNDED AS THE 'Golden Lion' brewery in 1862, Van Eecke has been owned for many years by the same family as the under-rated Leroy brewery of nearby Boezinge. But where Leroy concentrates on filtered, workmanlike, lighter ales and lagers, Van Eecke brews heavy beers for refermentation in large bottles and so on.

The Kapittel or 'Chapter' brands of abbey beer represent possibly the best range in Belgium. We have chosen just a couple to make the point. Picking particular ones led to interesting 'discussions' between the authors.

TASTING NOTES

As if to mock the Anglo-Saxon idiom that the heaviest beer in the range should be deep and dark, Kapittel Abt is amber-orange, with a thick, yellowish head that drops away. In the nose there is solvent beyond simply alcohol, plus fruit – prunes and citrus – and something spicy. The taste is dryish, with lots of liquorice, possibly from the Leroy yeast strain, which adds this as well as some coffee flavours. There is some spice too, giving the flavour of brandy poured on a sugar lump. The mouthfeel is quite dry, with a long-lasting impression of alcohol. There is not so much an aftertaste as a continuation of the above, with some throat-warming.

VERDICT

A great big grown-up barley wine, which ages well. Best enjoyed from a 75 cl bottle.

Brewery information   *See p. 120*

Inside a Van Eecke mash tun

BREWERY

Van Eecke

Kapittel Blond

6.5% alcohol by volume
beer style Blonde ale
33 cl bottles and on draught
importer James Clay & Sons; & Belgian Beer Import
importer Global Beer Network

EVERY BELGIAN BREWERY needs a work-a-day blond nowadays and this new addition to an old established range came as no big surprise. We are convinced that the faces of the monks on the labels of these beers are real people, as some kind of 'in joke'. Sadly neither of us are 'in' far enough to recognise them.

TASTING NOTES
Kapittel Blond is a clear yellow beer, with a white head that leaves nice lace. The nose gives hops, grain, and vague spiciness. If the basic taste is classical bitter-sweet, there is also a soft, slightly sour overtone that helps for an even better balance between hopping and malt base. Once again the alcohol is throat-warming. In the aftertaste, the malt sweetness dominates. Strangely, carbonation remains quite low.

VERDICT
The bottled and draught versions of this beer are, as far as we know, made from the same brew. However, it is clearly a superior drink from the bottle, especially when at room temperature. The draught version is better when cool, losing its refreshing qualities when warmer.

Brewery information *See p. 120*

BREWERY

Van Eecke

Kapittel Prior

9% alcohol by volume

Beer style Dubbel

33 cl & **75** cl bottles

UK importer James Clay & Sons; & Belgian Beer Import

US importer Global Beer Network

WE CAN ONLY assume that the decision to launch the Kapittel range back in 1946 had something to do with the launch of the village's other brewery, Sint-Bernardus (p. 108).

Originally, Prior was the top of the range and had a character more like Struise Brouwers' **Aardmonnik** (p. 113). Indeed, despite the acceptance of the term tripel as meaning a strong blond or golden beer, the original tripels, or XXX beers were dark brown in colour.

TASTING NOTES

Prior is deep brown with a reddish-orange sheen. Its huge, yellow-brownish head descends in rings, characteristic of this beer. A vinous nose of raisins, port wine and liquid rich fruit cake is there if you can sniff past the head! A taste of smoked wood and bitter hops are added to by the unsweetened liquorice that comes as a characteristic of the yeast strain. There is a lot of roasted malt. Nowadays it has lost its legendary slight sourness and the pronounced alcohol comes mainly in aged versions. The finish is a bit metallic, and the roasted bitterness gets even more pronounced.

VERDICT

Buy a case of 75 cl bottles, put it in your cellar and leave it be for three or four years. Younger versions, especially in smaller bottles can sometimes disappoint. 75 cl bottles that have been cellar-aged can be sensational. Thirty years ago this was dubbed 'champagne beer', long before others dared to try to use the term for another style of brew.

Van Eecke NV
Douvieweg 2, 8978 Watou
T 057 42 20 05   **F** 057 42 39 70
www.brouwerijvaneecke.tk

Group visits by arrangements only.
Next door to the brewery is a basic café called the **Brouwershof**, which opens every day from 09.00. Alternatively most of the beers brewed in Watou are available at the **Hommelhof** restaurant on the village square (17 Watouplein – **T** 057 38 80 24; **F** 057 38 85 90), where Stefan Couttenye practices the finer arts of cooking with beer, every day except Wednesday and lunchtimes only on Tuesday.

St. Louis Gueuze Fond Tradition

5% alcohol by volume

Beer style Gueuze

37.5 cl bottles only

Importer James Clay & Sons; & Belgian Beer Import

Importer Wetten Importers

WE WILL GET INTO TROUBLE for including this one. The Van Honsebrouck family are highly respected in the small world of Belgian brewing but even they get into trouble over this beer.

Van Honsebrouck beers are generally sweet and easy-drinking, or else strong but cosy. Their Fond Gueuze is none of these. Though this is not what bothers other brewers. The 'G' word does that.

You can only make gueuze using lambic, and lambic is a product of the region of Brussels and Payottenland. Ingelmunster is near Kortrijk, fully sixty kilometres to the west.

We do not know enough about the specific yeast culture used in the making of this and other St. Louis beers to give an expert opinion one way or the other, but the brewery's claim is that they use spontaneously fermented beer in the production of their beers, and so they say lambic and gueuze is what they are.

This little local spat had been irrelevant to serious beer drinkers as the St. Louis brands in question were all rather sweet and tacky beers. Then this one appeared.

TASTING NOTES

Unfiltered Fond Tradition has an orange yellow colour with a hazy, dense, white head. There is lactic acid and citrus in the nose, which rolls over into wet straw and something lambic-like, though not the idiomatic horse blanket. Sometimes it heads that way with additional aromas of nuts. The taste has citric, lemon-like acidity with some lactic. Muscat grape comes through retronasally. Little surprise that it has a truly refreshing, light mouthfeel, with a long citrus and buttermilk aftertaste.

VERDICT

While understanding exactly why the traditional lambic makers feel they should have a proper *appellation contrôlée* for their marvellous beers, it is difficult for us to exclude such an idiosyncratic beer from our listings, and not to note some similarities with the semi-protected species.

NV Brouwerij Van Honsebrouck
Oostrozebekestraat 43, 8770 Ingelmunster
T 051 33 51 60   **F** 051 31 38 39
E info@vanhonsebrouck.be
www.kasteelbier.be

Group tours by appointment only.
The brewery tap is the **Brouwershof**, a few doors down from the brewery. Most visitors prefer to go to the family's home of Ingelmunster Castle and drink in the moated **Kasteelkelder** (3 Kasteelstraat), which opens at 14.00 Saturday and Sunday all year round and Monday to Thursday from Easter to October. Most of the brewery's beers are available, some in a variety of vintages.

Saison de Pipaix

6% alcohol by volume

Beer style Saison

75 cl bottles only

UK importer Belgian Beer Import

US importer B. United International

THE SMALLER OF PIPAIX'S two breweries (see Dubuisson p. 53) is in the centre of the village and has been standing since 1785, though for part of that time it was derelict. Jean-Louis Dits took it over in 1984 with the deranged intention of recreating the original steam-powered brewery to make some traditional Age of Steam beers.

The result is part museum, part obsession, part commercial operation, though the latter is mainly to subsidise the dream. The secret ingredient of the stranger beers is lichen, which Jean-Louis swears he can justify by reference to old recipes found in the vaults of the brewery some years after he had taken over.

TASTING NOTES

Saison de Pipaix is usually red-amber in colour, hazy and with a medium yellowish-cream head. It has a fruity, near citrus nose that comes from its yeast. There might be iron there too. The taste is again yeast-laden, but filled in with grain, fruit and cookie malt. It all ends citrus and tart, and further enhanced by the carbonation. The beer is light to medium bodied. It is tart, fruity and sharp, with obvious dryness, and even some acid burn.

VERDICT

This is not a saison in the traditional hoppy mould. It is a beer that goes in phases, once spicy, then earthy and now rather subdued. Unique, mind.

Brewery information *See p. 123*

Vapeur en Folie

8% alcohol by volume

er style Saison

75 cl bottles only

mporter Belgian Beer Import

mporter B. United International

RECENT YEARS have seen Vapeur produce a couple of mainstream beers such as a light ale with vanilla, and **Cochonette**, a strong, pale blonde. It never used to be like this. Though not to the same extent as with Fantôme (p. 64) experts would debate whether this was a brewery of genius or one that had toppled over madness (Fr: *folie*).

TASTING NOTES

'Steaming Mad' is a golden ale with a fine haze and a good white head that leaves some lace. Various *fines herbes* can be detected in the nose – lemon grass and thyme maybe – plus apples and reminders of a farmyard – quite lovely, in some ways. Then it lunges into a completely different taste, more grainy with obvious malt and alcohol. At the back of the nose are spices made unrecognisable by residual sugar and again big alcohol. Initially refreshing, this loses out to the full-bodied sugar-malt onslaught and intoxicating punch.

VERDICT

This is a beer that starts subtle and ends like a sledgehammer. Forgivable, if heavy-handed.

Brasserie à Vapeur
Rue de Maréchal 1, 7904 Pipaix-Leuze
T 069 66 20 47   **F** 069 66 71 32
E brasserie@vapeur.com
www.vapeur.com

This deliciously eccentric old steam brewery opens a sampling room on site each Sunday from April to October opening at 11.00, and closing whenever seems appropriate. Ringing ahead to confirm is sensible, if only to find out whether there are eating possibilities. If there are, take them.

Echt Kriekenbier

6.8% alcohol by volume

Beer style Kriekenbier

33 cl bottles and occasionally on draught

UK importer Belgian Beer Import

US importer D&V International

THE CURRENT VERHAEGHE brothers are only the fourth generation of the family to run this brewery since it opened in 1880. They have managed to disprove two modern theories of management. The first is that business prowess leaks out of family firms with each new generation. The second is that brothers with different talents should never work together. This duet of thoughtful brewer and engaging salesman, make a great team.

Verhaeghe is a hybrid business – part brewery, part drinks suppliers. Hence, it makes lagers, ales and special beers for three largely separate markets. Only the special beers, variants on oak-aged ales, need bother us.

Cherry beers based on styles other than lambic must not, by Belgian law, be described as kriek but may be termed *kriekenbier*. Most of these are concoctions are dull brown beers to which cherry syrup has been added. We believe that Verhaeghe's Echt Kriekenbier is the only one made using whole cherries in a base of oud bruin ale.

TASTING NOTES

'Finest Cherry Beer' is a medium dark ruddy brown, with a fine, dense head of cream-pink hue. The obvious cherry nose is both fruity and woody, perfumed differently from the fresh fruit. Its taste is reassuringly tart, with a beautiful, almost extreme tannin background but again fruity – more so than in the nose. Retronasally there is a touch of fruit juice. There is an outspoken dry-out effect with huge amounts of organic acids. Given the nature of the beer, the taste is exactly where you want it to be.

VERDICT

An under-rated beer that suffers as a consequence of the awfulness of 'cherryade' beers from the lower leagues. Manages to be an authentic product and fun too.

Brewery information *See p. 125*

Verhaeghe

🍷 ## Vichtenaar

5.1% alcohol by volume

er style Aged brown ale

🍾 25 cl & 33 cl bottles

nporter Belgian Beer Import

nporter D&V International

IT WAS THE Verhaeghe brewery that first baulked the trend of phasing out their oak-aged ales – buying in and refurbishing oak tuns whenever they could. They also blend oak-aged ales for special customers.

A beautiful light quaffing beer called **Ouden Bruinen** (3.5% abv) failed to make it to these pages because TW is the only person living outside Vichte or under the age of 75 ever to have tried it. So did their fuller, sweeter, flagship beer, **Duchesse de Bourgogne**, albeit by a whisker. Vichtenaar is the family's own favourite.

TASTING NOTES
Under a huge, slightly irregular, beige head lurks a red-brown beer. In the nose there is a little acetic acid as wine vinegar, plus oak wood, brown malts and gingerbread. Although the first whiff is acetic, lactic acid arrives in its wake, along with something like fried sweet peppers. If that is what it is, it graces the taste too, which is less sharp than the nose leads one to expect. Wood and soft acids start to take over, along with faint flavours of chocolate, and lactates. Medium bodied, slightly chewy with some acid burn.

VERDICT
A good oud bruin, if a tad on the sweet side, with an acetic onslaught that is masked successfully.

NV Brouwerij Verhaeghe Vichte
Beukenhofstraat 96, 8570 Vichte
T 056 77 70 32   **F** 056 77 15 61
E brouwerij.verhaeghe@proximedia.be
www.brouwerijverhaeghe.be

Sadly this ancient brewery site is too much of a rambling maze for their liability insurers to allow public access.

None of the local cafés is reliable enough to recommend.

Walrave

Pick-Up Pils

4.8% alcohol by volume

Beer style Blond lager

25 cl bottles and on draught

UK importer This beer is not exported – it doesn't even get as far as Ghent!

US importer This beer is not exported to the US yet

THERE WAS QUITE SOME discussion before we decided to include this ordinary, if far from bad, Pilsener-style lager from an obscure brewery near Ghent. The town is known far more for its monumental castle than for the family brewery in its midst since 1862.

The beer revolution that hit Britain in the mid Seventies, had taken root in Belgium and the US by 1980 and then spread through most of the developed world and former European colonies, has passed by Laarne and Walrave.

Which serious brewery still claims that their beer should be consumed within a fortnight of purchase? Moral duty compels us to include them.

TASTING NOTES

The haze in Pick-Up Pils comes because nobody thought to centrifuge its flavours away. Its fluffy, dirty-white head leaves shards of lace. A grainy nose strikes one immediately, with straw and fresh yeast. Further, there is a marked sourish tang against background flavours of Kellogg's Corn Flakes and the freshest malt. Slightly sweet but herbal too. It is no more than light bodied, though the gristy slickness fills it out.

VERDICT

A surprising Pils – especially that slight sourness – but appealing nonetheless. OK, you can taste the sentimentality too, but a family-run brewery that eschews all publicity and would not even let us take photographs deserves respect. They should make more of this.

Brouwerij Walrave
Lepelstraat 36, 9270 Laarne
T 09 369 01 34

This is a possibly the shyest brewery in Belgium. No tours, no brewery tap and little presence beyond the town of Laarne.

Westmalle Dubbel Trappist

7% alcohol by volume
er style Dubbel
33 cl & 75 cl bottles and on draught
importer James Clay & Sons
importer Merchant du Vin

THE ABBEY OF Our Beloved Lady of the Sacred Heart at Westmalle was founded in 1794 by monks fleeing the French Revolution. In 1836 it was taken over by the Trappist Order and one of the first acts of the abbot, Dom Martinus, was to order the construction of a small brewery. The beers made there were not sold to the public until 1856 and even then on only an occasional basis at the abbey gates.

Proper commercialisation did not begin until the 1920s and even that was small scale. The beer was popular however and by the 1930s there was a real zest to be proper brewers.

Expansion is always a problem for a brewery that must by definition operate in a place of peace and contemplation. Breweries are noisy creatures. Somehow, Westmalle has managed it and still produces beers that manage to retain good quality. Long may this remain the case.

TASTING NOTES
Westmalle Dubbel can be a very lively beer. Dark amber to brown it sports ruby highlights, with a luxurious coat of yellow foam. Dark malts abound, perfumed and roasted, with touches of alcohol. Ageing brings with it vinous, nutty and raisin notes. In the taste, the dark malts reign again, this time with a bitter-roasted character. On warming, the stamp of brown sugar wells up. In the background, more flavours from pepper, marzipan and unfermented wort. There is something of English hops. Not only well-bodied but also well saturated. Swallowing warms the throat, while the aftertaste yields more marzipan, liquorice and a return of bitterness.

VERDICT
The great survivor. For all its obituarists, the original dubbel remains quietly entertaining.

Brewery information *See p. 129*

Westmalle Extra Trappist

5.5% alcohol by volume

Beer style Light ale

33 cl bottles only

UK importer This beer is never knowingly exported

US importer This beer is never knowingly exported

A COUPLE OF TIMES a year the brewery produces a light ale for the brothers and lay staff, which sometimes finds its way into the real world, for friends of the Order and maybe the Trappisten café (p. 129).

TASTING NOTES

[TW NOTES: as JPP is the only regular drinker of this beer not in a retreat, he could in fact write whatever he wants without much fear of contradiction. A pinch of salt may be required.]

Its creamy yellowish head, collapses slowly over a pale yellow beer with fading orange and green shades. Quite carbonated, the nose reeks of cream, malt, bread dough, fruit, nut and a bit of mould. The hop recipe was exempt from the accountant's savings plan. Iron and hop bitterness can be tasted in the head, while fresh white bread, aromatic hops and dried apple are in the body of the beer. Its bitterness is like hops mixed with walnut peel. Light bodied, it is at first creamy, then like mineral water. Its long bitter aftertaste makes it particularly refreshing.

VERDICT

JPP SAYS: Why include a beer you cannot find anywhere unless you take Holy Orders or by some minor miracle are at the brewery at an appointed hour, or chance upon some obscure pub in the Belgian countryside on a special day? Because this is the *ultimate* Belgian session beer, bearing witness as none other that Belgian top quality does not necessarily equate to lethal alcohol content.

TW SAYS: The idea that the ultimate session beer is found hidden behind cloistered walls for none but the most devout is one of the main reasons I love Belgium.

Brewery information *See p. 129*

BREWERY

Westmalle

☐ Westmalle Tripel Trappist

9.5% alcohol by volume

er style Tripel

　　　33 cl & **75** cl bottles

mporter James Clay & Sons

mporter Merchant du Vin

THE ABBEY AT WESTMALLE is said to have been responsible for creating one of the first pale tripel beers in 1936 or thereabouts and by that example to have led the move to designating such beers as being light in colour – with dubbel being brown. Whether or not this is entirely true, this beer is the one the other brewers want their beers to beat.

TASTING NOTES

Westmalle Tripel is a golden beer with a slight orange sheen when fresh, deepening to amber with age, its yellowish head remaining fine-bubbled. Grain, some chaff, and different pale malts rule the taste, with white candy sugar there too. Ageing brings more malt, then later port and Madeira notes, and eventually walnut. The first taste is of hops, followed briefly by scorched sugar if young. Gradually it acquires its more typical dry character, with high attenuation, the hallmark of the original pale tripel style. Oddly, ageing will sweeten the taste. In younger beer, the alcohol is marked, while age mellows this giving a creamier texture, with esters and fusels adding to the balance.

VERDICT

Westmalle Tripel remains seen in the Belgian brewing industry as the gold standard for such beers. Comparing this beer from various ages is an education in beer evolution and a rewarding experience.

Brouwerij Westmalle
Abdij der Trappisten van Westmalle
Antwerpsesteenweg 496, 2390 Malle
T 03 312 92 22　**F** 03 312 92 28
E info@trappistwestmalle.be
www.trappistwestmalle.be

The brewery may not be visited.
The nearest you will get is the **Trappisten** café, an enormous roadside tavern on the opposite side of the main road from the abbey (487 Antwerpsesteen-weg), catering mainly to day-trippers. It opens daily from 09.00 to 24.00. Last time we visited they offered to put grenadine in our Dubbel. Rather than weep publicly, we sat in silent prayer.

Trappist Westvleteren 8°

8% alcohol by volume

Beer style Dubbel

33 cl bottles only

UK importer This brewery's beers are never officially exported

US importer This brewery's beers are never officially exported

SINT SIXTUS' ABBEY dates from 1831 and its brewing activities from 1839.

We thought long and hard before including them in this book. In 2005, an American website made great play of the fact that one of the abbey's beers – we forget which – had been voted 'the best beer in the world'. To be fair to the website the story got more coverage in Belgium and internationally than they could reasonably have foreseen, but either way regrettable events followed.

The country lanes round Westvleteren became crammed with cars, their owners queuing up for a 'must buy' case of this great new discovery that had lain ignored in their midst for years. Fights broke out as supplies dried up. This proved that the beer was worth having. Why would people fight over a simple beer? They are not stupid, or greedy, or easily led, surely?

A more realistic truth is that these are pretty good beers but none of them is best in class, let alone a contender for 'best beer in the world'. Rather, they tell a nice story of monastic brewing in a quiet rural setting, and of Sundays spent cycling out into the flatlands for a glass of something in simple but pleasant surroundings.

A bit of romantic nonsense adds hugely to the taste of a beer.

TASTING NOTES

The 8 sports a thick, beige head that collapses slowly over a dark brown beer with a burgundy sheen. In aged beers this goes fast amid a cola-like bubbling. The nose explodes with chocolate, roasted malts, ripe pears, mocha, faint hops and summer haystacks, while older beers are sweeter, with molasses, lactate, vintage port and hazelnuts. Tasting gives a little bitterness at first, mainly from roasted and burnt malts, rather than hops. Although hugely malty the beer is much less sweet than expected, with additional flavours of walnut peel, black coffee and chicory. Ageing adds some bitterness but with a fine, spritzy, acid-like surround, the beer becoming fruity with black wine grapes, hazelnuts, dried plums and figs. It is a chewy beer, with low carbonation when young, lasting bitterness and some residual sugar. The older beer is less dense but more refined and even thirst-quenching. In the aftertaste is sweetness in abundant, alcoholic tones.

VERDICT

A well-made, dense beer that is virtually indestructible and mellows with the years. The beer is sometimes known as Extra. When young the beer is a crude, uncut diamond, while in ageing it shines brilliantly.

Brewery information See p. 132

Trappist Westvleteren 12°

0.2% alcohol by volume

eer style Strong abbey-style ale

33 cl bottles only

mporter This brewery's beers are never officially exported

mporter This brewery's beers are never officially exported

THE WESTVLETEREN website gives details of how to order a case of beer in advance. At the time of going to press, their phone line was generally jammed with calls from cafés, beer agencies and members of the public, many trying to make a buck by sourcing a nice cheap case of something to sell on at a huge mark-up. Squalid, really.

The Order has asked for suggestions as to how to combat the problem. We have suggested two ways.

The first is to hike the price through the roof until this demand goes down, perhaps explicitly marking on the invoices the increased donation that goes to charitable works.

The second is simply to stop selling the beer anywhere other than at the **In de Vrede** (p. 132) and hold back stocks of the 8 and 12 to age peacefully for a while before being supplied to selected customers at a suitably marked up price.

TASTING NOTES

Westvleteren 12 is a dark brown beer with a deep reddish sheen and a luxurious, thick brown head. The nose tells of dark malts, blue cheese, wood and restrained hops. Ageing gives creaminess, dried dark plums, chocolate, and biscuity caramelisation. Left even longer, port and Madeira character, raisins and more chocolate come. Roasted dark malts rule the taste. Young beers are excessively sweet. Ageing deepens the flavours with biscuit, *crème de noix*, walnut oil and dried fruit. Wait longer and old sweet Sauternes, vintage sherry, and dark, ripe fruit emerge. A chewy, complex beer even when young, later alcohol and fusels deepen the impression. Its long lasting aftertaste yields chocolate and fulfilment.

VERDICT

This beer, sometimes known as Abt, should have no 'best before' date. In a sensible world, it would be produced in dated batches with a high premium accruing to the best vintages.

Brewery information *See p. 132*

🍷 Trappist Westvleteren Blond

5.8% alcohol by volume

Beer style   Pale ale

🍾   **33** cl bottles only

UK importer   This brewery's beers are never officially exported

US importer   This brewery's beers are never officially exported

UNTIL 2000 or thereabouts the lighter of the Westvleteren beers was a 6% abv dark beer with a red cap. In the way of rare things in the beer world it was hailed as excellent. It would have been rude to say otherwise.

Christianity's 2000th anniversary coincided with some major changes in the world of Trappist brewing, the smallest of which was the replacement of that 6% beer with this rather nice light-coloured one, with a natty green top.

TASTING NOTES

Westvleteren Blond is a pale golden ale with gentle head that laces well. At first, the nose is grainy, followed by a thick cloud of hop aroma. The taste is beautifully hoppy, not as in an overloaded American IPA but more as in a fine, traditional Kentish cask ale. There are raisins in the aroma but none of the sweetness of dried fruit. The mouthfeel is non-descript but there is alcohol, even though this is a modest blonde. The aftertaste gives another impression of hops again, though recently the hoppiness seems to have been wilfully restrained in favour of a fuller body with more grain.

VERDICT

On its day this beer is an absolute delight, though it must be said that it is variable. What varies most is its sometimes exquisite, occasionally just leaden hopping, which is ironic considering the brewery is based in Belgium's main hop-growing area.

*Light snacks and the abbey's brews at the **In de Vrede**, the café-cum-conference centre opposite the abbey.*

Brouwerij Westvleteren
Sint Sixtus Trappistenbdij
Donkerstraat 12, 8640 Westvleteren
T 057 40 10 57   **F** 057 40 14 20
E brouwerij@sintsixtus.be
www.sintsixtus.be

The brewery cannot be visited.
There is a huge café-cum-conference centre opposite the abbey gates, called **In de Vrede** (or 'Inn of Peace'), which is open every day except Thursday (October to March) and Friday (all year) from 10.00, tending to close by 20.00 between November and March. This rather elegant barn serves light snacks and the abbey's brews in a reliably calm atmosphere. Nowadays it is often the only place you will find these beers.

Beyond Belgian

NO WE DO NOT MEAN 'Beyond Belgium'. The heading is deliberate.

When the late Michael Jackson began writing about the excellence of Belgian beers in the 1970s, the world had just started to re-acquaint itself with the idea that beer could be good, or even stylish. In those days, to say that you preferred beer to wine was to court disgrace. It ranked somewhere between saying you loved someone of the same sex, reckoning Buddhism was cool, or choosing to shop at open air markets.

Times change, and with them our aspirations.

The appreciation of and enthusiasm for Belgian beers grew steadily in many parts of the world. Inevitably among the enthusiasts came some who wanted to try making these beers for themselves. Over time the term 'Belgian-style' began to appear on the labels of brews that had no connection with the country.

Sitting in a fashionable beer boudoir in Manhattan one sunny late autumn afternoon in 1997, the editor of what was then the *Good Beer Guide to Belgium & Holland* dropped his role into the conversation – generally a reliable tactic for reducing the bar bill and used without scruples back then.

The barman, upset perhaps by the reverence being shown by his regulars to this stranger, deployed generosity and bonhomie to their full lethal potential. Turning the label of a tall, brown, shouldered, 75 cl bottle away from view, he poured out a goblet of amber-brown foaming strong ale 'on the house', saying something like, "How do you rate this brewery then?"

Honour on the line, the editor tried his best. The beer tasted something like Maredsous 8 or old-style Gauloise, or maybe Moinette Brune ... no, something from Sterkens ... or was that Van Eecke ...

Floundering set in and was obvious to all.

The barman assisted with a harpoon of effortless rescue, "It's from Cooperstown, in upstate New York."

"Really? So where do they import it from?"

"Nowhere. They make it there."

Belgian beer lovers had some new friends. And Belgian brewers had a new problem.

That beer was called Ommegang and although it was not the first 'Belgian' beer to emanate from a foreign brewery, it was at that time the most obviously accomplished.

Not all who trod the path of those Cooperstown brewers have been as impressive in their recreation of the classic Belgian styles, of course. But nobody foresaw that within a decade a new breed of brewer would emerge, in the US and elsewhere.

Inspired and informed by the authentic practitioners of the great Belgian arts they may have been, but these newer brewers were not awed by them. Instead they took several steps further down a path where even the most adventurous Belgian brewers had yet to tread.

Allagash Curieux

9.5% alcohol by volume

Beer style Tripel

75 cl bottles and on draught

UK importer This beer is not imported to the UK yet

US availability Across 20 States

IN 1995, BREWER ROB TOD, spotting a gap in the US microbrewery market, began to produce a Belgian-style wheat beer, called **Allagash White**. It gained a cult following in its home state of Maine and its fame soon spread. Standards have never fallen.

A dubbel and a tripel followed, along with a spiced winter brew called **Grand Cru** and a just-plain-strong ale called **Allagash Four**.

By 2004, the time had come to play. Rob took advantage of a generously loopy American law that forbids the re-use of oak bourbon casks, and bought some in which to re-ferment his tripel for six weeks. Curieux was born, the first of seven beers from Allagash, thus far, that age in oak in some form.

The more recent beers are forging a new path for the brewery, allowing lateral thinking to shape new styles of beer for the next part of the American Revolution in beer. Curieux perhaps marks the highest point of the old world Belgian base from which Allagash took off into the new world ways, referencing but no longer mimicking Belgian practice.

TASTING NOTES

Allagash Curieux is a pale yellow-orange beer, crowned with a reticent, transparent head. It has a beautiful Bourbon nose, restrained to create a good balance with subtle spiciness and chalk. Its taste is sweet, vinous and alcoholic with a serious punch. It remains malty despite the additional lagering. The mouthfeel is powerful and burning, yet not aggressive. Despite the Bourbon influence, it is definitely complex in a layered way that goes far beyond the simple addition of alcohol and vanilla-wood touches.

VERDICT

This is the best we have tasted from Allagash, where brewmaster Rob Tod, no longer awed by Belgian traditions, is creating his own.

Allagash Brewing Company
50 Industrial Way, Portland, ME 04103, USA
T 001 207 878 5385   **E** info@allagash.com
www.allagash.com

Tours of the brewery happen daily, Monday to Friday at 15.00.

Port Brewing (California, USA)

 ## Cuvée de Tomme

11% alcohol by volume

beer style Kriekenbier

 37.5 cl & **75** cl bottles and occasionally on draught

importer This beer is not exported to the UK yet

availability California, Arizona, Washington, Pennsylvania and Massachusetts

THE SOLANA BEACH PIZZA PORT BREWERY was started in 1992 by Vince and Gina Marsaglia, who remain owners of a much-expanded company, now based in the old Stone Brewing set-up at San Marcos. In the old days they could turn out up to seven barrels of beer a week. Nowadays capacity is nearer a hundred.

The key component in this success is one Tomme Arthur, Director of Brewing Operations, a man much festooned with awards for his flavoursome beers and a key player in the Californian wing of the great American beer revival. In fact he is so important that he gets to create his own Cuvée a couple of times a year. This is it.

Its massive brown ale base is made from malted barley, raisins, candy sugar and sour cherries. It is fully fermented before being placed in Bourbon barrels where it ages for a further year, inoculated with more sour cherries and wild Brettanomyces yeast.

TASTING NOTES

The colour of this beer is reminiscent of how **Liefmans Kriek** used to be, dark-red with a deep sheen of old burgundy. Overwhelmingly the nose is composed of old cherries, fresh cherry pie, and *boerejongens* (or cherry jenever) – including the alcohol! Further aromas are of old oak, mixed fruit, liquorice and old, farm-made Slivovitz. Its taste is sweet but within a frame of sour fruit. Found fresh and on draught, additional cherry is unmistakable and goes well with the underlying dryish, alcoholic *triple*. Chocolate and vinous touches make it like Viennese cherry cake. In the aftertaste the *boerejongens* lingers on and on.

VERDICT

A unique and world-beating beer of huge complexity, made possible by the combined thinking of generations of long gone Belgian brewers with that of some very-much-alive Californians.

[JPP NOTES: Their L.A. Angels' Share is none too bad either.]

Port Brewing Company
155 Mata Way, Suite # 104, San Marcos, CA, USA
T 1 800 918 6816 (US only)   **F** none
E via website
www.portbrewing.com

This brewery and its sister operation, the Lost Abbey, share a tasting room in which, for a fee, the brewers will lead you through an appreciation of a range of their beers. This is open on Fridays from 16.00 to 20.00 and on Saturdays from 12.00 to 17.00. Brewery tours are available as part of the tasting room experience. Groups should book in advance.

Supplication

7% alcohol by volume

Beer style Kriekenbier

 37.5 cl bottles and on draught

UK importer This beer is not exported to the UK yet

US availability California and Pennsylvania

THE ORIGINAL RUSSIAN RIVER Brewing Company was set up in 1997 by a firm that managed Champagne cellars. They employed the wine making son of a wine making family, Vinnie Cilurzo, as its first brewer. A decade later, RRBC looks like a microbrewery with a decent wine cave within it – though those oak casks have beers not wines maturing inside them.

Vinnie and wife Natalie bought the business in 2002 and nowadays need all those barrel ends as somewhere to nail all their plaques and awards – 'Small Brewing Company of the Year', 'Small Brewing Company Brewmaster of the Year', 'Large Brewpub of the Year' and just plain 'Brewery of the Year' to name a few.

At the last count RRBC made just over thirty different beers in the course of a year and lead the way in oak-aged beers on the West coast, of which five are in regular production. We have chosen the oak-aged brown ale as the representative from a high quality range. As with Allagash, (p. 136), these are beers that give the term 'Belgian style' a whole new meaning.

Brown Ale Aged in Oak Barrels with Cherries Added

Refermented in the Bottle

TASTING NOTES

Supplication is a reddish-orange, cloudy beer with a fine, slightly pink, dense head. Cherries and old wine seem to explode out of the glass, delivering an unbelievably inviting and exotic smell with impressions of Bulgar yoghurt and lots of vintage Burgundy. Sour fruit, cherries, vanilla, velvety Brettanomyces and *lactobacillus* strains vie as in the best gueuzes for domination. The flavour of old Burgundy returns retronasally. Lactic acid, fruit acids, oak and vanilla accompany each other, while on top of all this is a velvety, rich texture, like drinking yoghurt.

VERDICT

The nearest American attempt yet at doing something lambic.

Russian River Brewing Company
725 4th Street, Santa Rosa, CA 95404
T 001 707 545 2337   **F** 001 707 545 2338
E info@russianriverbrewing.com
www.russianriverbrewing.com

Russian River is fortunate in having its production facility alongside a large brewpub, which opens daily at 11.00, through to 01.00 on Friday and Saturday and midnight the rest of the week. Happy hour operates from 16.00 to 18.00 Monday to Thursday and all day Sunday.

New Belgium Brewing (Colorado, USA)

La Folie

7% alcohol by volume

beer style Aged brown ale

75 cl bottles only

importer This beer is not exported to the UK yet

availability Limited release across those 18 States between the Mississippi and the Pacific Ocean that are supplied by the brewery

BACK IN 1991 Jeff Lebesch returned from a cycling trip across Belgium with a great idea for a brewery. With wife Kim Jordan doing the marketing and, a while later, Belgian brewer Peter Bouckaert, formerly of Rodenbach (p. 96) and a short-lived Belgian micro called Zwingel, they have made it happen in Colorado.

Their biggest hit has been **Fat Tire**, an attractive, light, amber ale that has permeated tap rooms across the whole of the western United States. They make a pretty good pass at a witbier, a dubbel and a tripel too. But it is the tiny production seeping from Peter Bouckaert's little indulgence that has really caught the imagination.

La Folie may 'closely resemble a Belgian lambic' according to the Denver Post, but we reckon it bears more than a passing resemblance to something rather more oaky from the region of West Flanders, home of one Rodenbach brewery.

TASTING NOTES

La Folie is a dark brown beer with orange highlights, the yeast suspension making it cloudy. Its thick, brownish head disappears fast. The nose is extreme vintage wine, with tones of oak wood, acetic and lactic acids, plus a jumble of esters. The mouth detects acetic acid but there are lemon-like tones contributing to a half-expected, expressly sour sensation, though the acidic onslaught fades to a fruitier taste – blue grape, orange rind and sherry. Each batch is different – they have only a few tuns here for blending. Some are indeed gueuze-like, while others are more Pinot Noir. Tannin-rich, woody and even a bit resinous, they can reach enviable complexity. The acid makes the beer seem thinner than it is. The oak-ripened vinous taste goes on and on.

VERDICT

A little bit of old Flanders being recreated in New Belgium.

New Belgium Brewing Company
500 Linden, Fort Collins, CO 80524
T 1 888 622 4044 (US only)
E nbb@newbelgium.com
www.newbelgium.com

There are guided and self-guided tours every day from Tuesday to Saturday between 10.00 and 18.00, with free beer tastings.

Panil Barriquée Sour

8% alcohol by volume

Beer style Aged brown ale

 75 cl bottles only

UK importer This beer is not exported to the UK yet

US importer Shelton Brothers

THE BREWERY at Torrechiara, near Parma, where the ham comes from, is part of an impressive revival of brewing in Italy that has seen nearly a hundred microbreweries and brewpubs open up in the last two decades. What singles this one out for mention is that in among the stainless steel, pristine clean surfaces that are the hallmark of any modern brewery is a small collection of oak tuns, in which its sharp, sour mixer beer ferments away.

In clear deference to the traditions of Dutch-speaking northern Europe, Dr Renzo Losi has created an old-fashioned stock ale for blending. In the tradition of a Flemish oak-aged oud bruin ale, it is bottled in its neat, unsweetened form as Panil Barriquée (or barrel-aged Panil).

TASTING NOTES

This is a brown-coloured beer with a clear reddish sheen. The head is brown with a pink tinge. The nose comes with old oak, wood stain, cherry cake and chocolate, as well as lactate and wafts of something akin to Brettanomyces. The taste conveys a hint of diacetyl, a good trace of bitter chocolate, lots of tannin and multiple sour fruits such as lemon and its rind. Retronasally a bitter taste emerges, with a metallic tang and a touch of phenol. The body is difficult to assess, going from thinnish from the acidity to fuller from the weight of the beer. There are fusels there and eventually brandy-like notes. Aptly for an Italian beer the texture is of Balsamico vinegar. As an aftertaste comes something reminiscent of nougat.

VERDICT

Panil Barriquée is easily one of the most complex beers we have ever tasted, the nose being simply phenomenal. Early versions seem to have acted as chemical extractors of all that was in the wood. However, it is uncompromisingly bold and cocks a snook to all who are afraid of outspoken tastes. In being completely unsweetened it poses a question without an answer.

Birrificio Torrechiara
Strada Pilastro 35, 43013 Torrechiara, Italy
T 0521 355113   **F** 0521 355136
E ufficio@panilbeer.com
www.panilbeer.com

We have no details about brewery visits or nearby cafés.

How to create a beer cellar

WITH VERY FEW EXCEPTIONS, beers that are best when fresh have been poorly made.

Unless it has been pasteurised, beer is a living product. It appreciates a bit of time to settle down and start working to improve itself. The best way to let it do this is to do nothing, safely.

Whether seeking to offer your restaurant customers a beer list that is as good as the wine list, or simply keeping your home stocked with a few fun beers to keep you and your house guests amused on winter evenings, creating a beer cellar is as sensible a project as it is simple to deliver.

Which beers are worth cellaring?

We are only considering bottled beers here. Draughts beers are complicated. Canned beers are dead – they do not mature, they fade.

As with wines and people, beers age with varying degrees of gracefulness. Though as with cheeses (and people), the point at which peak quality is reached is in part a matter of taste.

The rough rules to inform a best guess, in descending order of reliability, include:

- Stronger beers (8% alcohol by volume and above) age better than those of ordinary strength, because alcohol is a preservative
- Beers bottled with yeast mature more obviously than filtered beers
- The darker the glass of the bottle, the better the beer inside is protected
- Beer matures better in larger bottles (75cl and over) than in smaller ones
- Brown ales tend to age better than blonde
- Lambics keep longer than ales, which keep longer than lagers
- Highly hopped beers are preserved well for six to nine months then go 'skunky'
- Beers made with fruit syrups or a high amount of non-malt sugars age poorly

Most Belgian beers now state a 'Best before' date on their labels to reduce some of the guesswork, though bureaucratic restrictions have rendered these virtually meaningless for those beers that age the best. Some makers of authentic gueuze argue, with justification, that their best beers should have 'Best after' dates.

What do you need in a beer cellar?

Beer in storage does not like sunlight, so keep it away from your beer cellar.

Freezing a beer will denature it beyond recovery. Beer will tolerate temperatures as low as 1°C (34°F) but develops noticeably slower below 8°C (46°F). So, avoiding extreme low temperature is essential. Keeping the cellar temperature at a minimum of 8°C is perfectionist territory.

Raising the beer's temperature above body heat – to 40°C (104°F) – will do strange things to its yeast, causing bizarre changes to the taste. Above 12°C (54°F) yeast activity rises, the beer ages faster and more crudely, though again many beers can tolerate this. So, avoid extreme high temperatures but do not worry too much about the effect of a few sunny days. Keeping the cellar temperature falsely low rarely makes sense.

Some beers in corked bottles can 'cork', or oxidise, in the same way as wines, if the cork dries out or splits. However, CO_2 produced by active refermentation offers some protection.

Most corks used for Belgian beers are nowadays made from compounded cork that does not dry out, though it can add to the opposite problem, which is build up of pressure, especially if the beer has been stored in warmer conditions.

Beers in capped bottles should be stored upright.

Some people store corked bottles on their side, though the rationale of this is scientifically dubious. It can also lead to serving problems as sediment collecting down the side of the bottle will make it difficult to pour a clear beer, should you be seeking to do that.

There is no need to obsess about humidity.

In practice, JPP has a partially underground cellar, while TW uses his garage. In practice, neither of us has experienced many problems, except when we have chosen to stock the wrong beers.

What do you put into your cellar?

Of course the bottom line calculations must be based on what you can source, how long it will keep and how frequently you are likely to drink it.

Belgium itself is awash with beer warehouses (Du: *drankhandel*; Fr: *depot*) that are open to the public. These vary in the extent to which they carry special beers. The best are listed in the *Good Beer Guide Belgium* (CAMRA Books).

British residents can bring back as much beer as they like 'for personal consumption' from Belgian warehouses and shops, as this will have included local tax. In practice HM Customs & Excise will accept a figure of up to 100 litres per head.

Most of the beers in this book are imported to both the UK and the US, via importers who have reliable transport and storage facilities. The trick is to find a local beer store that you trust to have continued storing it well at the next stage of the supply chain.

What do you take out of your cellar?

The best temperature at which to serve a fine ale is 8° to 12°C (46° to 54°F) – the historical meaning of 'room temperature' (Du: *kamertemperatuur*; Fr: *temperée* or *chambrée*). This allows for a little warming while it is being enjoyed.

The main reason that lesser beers are served cold is so as to take away the foul tastes found in many when at a temperature that maximises their flavour. Try this with a few well known international lager brands and you will see what we mean.

Served cold, ales lose much of their character, as the esters that make up many of the most prominent flavour chemicals become inactive. Storing cold is not a problem, but try to allow time for the beer to reach room temperature before serving.

One tip for a hot summer's day. Beers that are slightly acidic, such as oak-aged ales or authentic gueuze and kriek, cooled to 4°C (39°F) or lower, make far more refreshing drinks than even the best lagers. Sacrilegious but fun.

Yeast sediment in a beer will take a minimum of four days and possibly up to two weeks to 'drop bright' so even if your beers are not being set aside for cellaring, they will not reach peak presentation immediately on delivery.

Some beers, such as unfiltered wheat beers are not intended to drop bright, as the haze in these is fine wheat flour. Indeed, if they have, it may be a sign that they are past their best. Wheat beers do not gain much from cellar ageing so fast throughput is usually a better solution.

Belgians of the old school will pour out all bar the last centimetre of their beer from the bottle, swilling the rest and emptying its contents into the last mouthful of beer in their glass to get 'the goodness' of the yeast. The finesse of experience? Or confirmation of the eccentricity of Belgians? You be the judge.

An appreciation of the difference between the effects of a 'beautiful infection' such as brettanomyces *lambicus* slow yeast and a foul infection due to contaminated yeast or other poor practice, takes a lifetime to acquire. If it smells agricultural or musty, keep an open mind, if it smells like a harbour or canal, send it back.

TEN TOP TIPS FOR RESTAURATEURS

1. Any decent wine cellar will be fine for keeping beers that benefit from cellaring.

2. The best temperature at which to serve a top quality bottled ale is 8° to 12° C (46° to 54°F).

3. Open the bottle at the table, unless experience suggests that this particular case is a tad explosive, in which case bringing the beer ready-poured is better etiquette than drowning the customer. Always leave the bottle on the table for inspection.

4. For sediment beers, pour most of the contents in one go, as clear as possible, leaving one centimetre of beer in the bottom of the bottle. This gives the customer the option of pouring the remainder into the glass if they wish. The same rule applies when serving beers from 75cl bottles, which are intended for sharing between two to four people.

5. Sharing 75cl bottles of different beers with different courses is considerably easier than with wines and may inspire the chef to find good pairings with particular dishes. *Cuisine à la bière* is becoming a popular option in Belgian restaurants and gastropubs.

6. Belgian beers come with their own glasses for marketing, not quality reasons. Served in a regular pint or half-pint beer mug or jug, Belgian beers tend to look tacky. Served in large, balloon-style wine glasses, filled three-quarters full with liquid, they often present even better than in their 'official' glass.

7. A traditional gueuze or kriek is best served in a tall glass with straight diagonal sides. When served as an aperitif, consider champagne flutes.

8. That old line about beer and wine not mixing is wrong – it is the total volume of alcohol that 'makes you feel queer'.

9. What *is* true is that female palates are less drawn to bitter beers than male, that wine drinkers tend to appreciate authentic gueuze and oak-aged ales more readily than traditional ale drinkers and that people who never dreamed they would like beer of any kind often surprise themselves by finding pleasure in some obscure Belgian brew.

10. There is no such thing as a craftsman quality Belgian draught lager.

UK beer importers

THE UK MARKET in beer is both parochial and global. The British are not great at enjoying the products of other beer cultures but on the other hand have sat idly by while the vast bulk of the UK brewing industry has been packaged up and sold into foreign ownership.

As a result, most beer imported to the UK consists of some other country's take on dull blond lager with an eye-catching label.

However, there exists a small but growing band of more adventurous importers, who specialise in sourcing and stocking characterful beers from the world's better craft breweries. Most are small-scale and operate in a world where exclusive import and distribution deals are impossible to police and honoured more in the breach.

These are the people who licensed trade customers should go to for orders by the case or barrel. For a list of where to buy Belgian beers locally, see the *Good Beer Guide Belgium* (CAMRA Books).

If your local beer shop or pub specialising in foreign beers is not sure where to go to get a favourite beer for you, point them in the direction of the companies on this list.

Beer Direct

10 Ferndale Close
Werrington
Stoke-on-Trent ST9 0PW
T&F 01782 303823
E sales@beerdirect.co.uk
www.beerdirect.co.uk

Small enough to be friendly and approachable but big enough to offer distribution throughout most of England and Wales to trade customers. As well as the breweries mentioned in the text, they import directly from Ecaussinnes, Lefèbvre, Roman and Van Steenberge. Beers from around thirty other Belgian breweries can be sourced.

Belgian Beer Import

PO Box 810
Woking GU21 4WF
T 01483 740984   F 01483 740984
E bartverhaeghe@btconnect.com
www.belgianbeerimport.org.uk

In London and the South East, as far north as Peterborough and Leicester, this is the place for bars and off-licenses to contact for an amazing wholesale range of Belgian beers – about 150 in all. They will trunk large enough orders elsewhere too. As well as the beers and breweries highlighted in the text, they can source beers from many other Belgian breweries, including Achilles, Alvinne, Angerik', de Bie', Binchoise', Bockor, du Bocq, Boelens', Bosteels, Caulier, De Block, 't Gaverhopke, Géants-Ellezelloise', de Graal', Grain d'Orge', Oud Beersel, Silenrieux' and Silly, among others.

Bierlijn

E hughbierlijn@planet.nl

www.bierlijn.com

Pronounced 'Beer-Line' – the popular saviours of many a beer festival organiser's sanity. Small Anglo-Dutch company based in the Netherlands and shipping beers both ways across the North Sea. They supply much of the classier beer to Belgian Beer Import, with whom they work closely. Will supply direct if the order is 60 cases or more. Beer festivals a speciality. They supply the starred' beers on BBI's additionals list (above).

Cave Direct

Unit B10, Larkfield Trading Estate

New Hythe Lane

Larkfield

Kent ME20 6SW

T 01622 710339

E info@beermerchants.com

www.beermerchants.com

Although Cave Direct will deal directly with any private customer, most of their sales are to the licensed trade. They will deliver orders of 10 cases or more anywhere in the UK – smaller in or around the M25. They reckon to be able to source beers from over fifty Belgian breweries, especially longer established independents, importing most to order.

James Clay & Sons

Unit 1, Grove Mills

Elland

West Yorkshire HX5 9DZ

T 01422 377560   F 01422 375100

E info@jamesclay.co.uk

www.beersolutions.co.uk

Wholesale beer merchant and importer, founded in 1982 and dealing with trade customers over much of England and Wales. As well as the breweries mentioned in the text, they import directly from Bosteels, Halve Maan, Liefmans and Timmermans. They can also source beers from another thirty or so Belgian breweries.

Shelton Brothers UK Ltd

31 St Loyes House

St Loyes Street

Bedford MK40 1ZL

T 0787 986 8602   F 0788 463 7661

E markpayne@talk21.com

The Shelton Brothers have played a huge role in the success of the best Belgian brewers in the US. Now they are dipping a toe in the UK pond, hoping to bring to the UK import market some American-style business discipline and pizzazz.

US beer importers

THE US IS, as we all know, a model society when it comes to free enterprise. Or so you may think, until you take a careful look at the arcane three-tier system that applies to the buying and selling of imported foreign beers.

The way it works is this. Importers may import beers but are not allowed to sell them directly to beer stores or the general public. Rather they must sell them only to distributors, who themselves are not allowed to sell directly to the public.

The distributors may sell on to retailers, who are the only people allowed to sell to the general public.

At each step in this process those who play their part have legitimate expenses to recoup and a living to make. This puts at least three expensive steps between the foreign beer-maker and the US customer drinking their beer.

It is a hang-on from Prohibition and a sop to those who believe that alcohol is the devil's work, sent by evil-doers to corrupt the innocent. It also explains why Belgian-brewed beer, even if brewed by or for a Christian religious order, can be pretty expensive in North America.

The upside is that many of the importers have taken the view that with such an expensive system imposed on them, they may as well focus on marketing the very best beers, so much so that they have had to persuade some brewers to go an extra mile.

There are now upwards of a dozen examples of US importers going directly to Belgian brewers and commissioning top quality craft beers that were not currently on the Belgian market. Some remain so, which does not always go down well with Belgian beer lovers, who sometime feel deprived of a great treat that should be theirs.

For each and every beer we list, we have tried to trace the company that held the import contract (if any) to the US at the time that we went to press, in order that customers can tell their suppliers where to source them as easily as possible.

Artisanal Imports Inc.
PO Box 41029, Austin, TX 78704
T (512) 440 0811   F (512) 440 0884
E info@artisanalimports.com
www.artisanalimports.com

A fairly recent edition to the importing world but handling Sint-Bernardus' Grottenbier brands, big bottles of St. Feuillien and Bosteels too.

Belukus Marketing Inc.
3304 Longmire Drive, College Station, TX 77845
T (979) 680 8590   F (979) 680 8594
E brad@belukus.net
www.belukus.net

Going since the early Nineties, this Texas-based operation handles a small number of larger independent Belgian, British and German breweries. As well as De Koninck and Malheur, it handles Lefèbvre and Liefmans. Distributes to 41 States.

B. United International Inc.
PO Box 661, Redding, CT 06896
T (203) 938 0713   F (203) 938 1124
E bunitedint@hotmail.com
www.bunitedint.com

Founded in 1995 and specialising in importing beers and other light drinks for onward sale to distributors in 39 States. As well as the breweries listed they also deal with Alvinne, and independent breweries from Britain, Germany, Switzerland, Italy, Scandinavia, South Africa and Japan.

D&V International Inc.
4452 Royal Fern Way, Palm Beach Gardens FL 33410
T (561) 622 7581   F (561) 799 6648
E darius@specialtybeer.com
www.specialtybeer.com

Specialist Belgian beer importer that tends to go for established independents rather than new micros. Sells on to distributors in 39 States at present. As well as the breweries listed they also deal with Binchoise and Oud Beersel.

Duvel Moortgat USA Ltd.

21 Railroad Avenue #32, Cooperstown, NY 13326
T (607) 544 1800   F (607) 544 1801
E info@duvelusa.com
www.duvelusa.com

Duvel Moortgat is so successful in the US market
that it now handles its own imports of Duvel
Moortgat and its subsidiary Achouffe, through a
site close to the Ommegang brewery, in which it
also holds a major stake.

Global Beer Network

PO Box 2069, Santa Barbara, CA 93120
T (800) 442 3379   T (805) 967 8111
F (805) 805 683 1470
E global@globalbeer.com
www.globalbeer.com

The Californian beer importer that first persuaded
Bavik to bottle their Aged Pale neat. As well as the
breweries listed they also deal with Boelens, Halve
Maan, Roman, Silenrieux, Silly and Van Steenberge.
Currently sells to distributors in 33 States on the
East and West coasts plus the mid-West.

Manneken-Brussel Importers Inc.

1305 West Oltorf Street, Suite # 100
Austin, TX 78704
T (512) 385 2188   F (512) 512 385 2122
E info@mbibeer.com
www.mbibeer.com (under construction)

Importers of Chimay beers. Sells to distributors
throughout the US.

Merchant du Vin

18200 Olympic Avenue South
Tukwila, WA 98188-4721
T (253) 656 0320   F (253) 253 872 5530
E info@mdvbeer.com

Merchant du Vin-East

449 Pittsfield Lenox Road, Suite 201
Lenox, MA 01240
T (413) 443 4868   F (413) 443 4514
www.merchantduvin.com

Founded in 1978 by wine importer Charles Finkel,
this bespoke agency imports beers from three
Trappist breweries and Lindemans. Sells to
distributors throughout the US.

Shelton Brothers

PO Box 486, Belchertown, MA 01007
T (413) 253 0500   F (413) 253 0600
E info@sheltonbrothers.com
www.sheltonbrothers.com

Is there such a concept as importers with
attitude? Brothers Dan, Will and Joel Shelton
have created a business based on importing an
elite list of craft beers to the US from across the
known brewing world and beyond. Even to make
it to the Shelton list is a sign of greatness. They
are clearly passionate about the brewers they
represent, way beyond any intention to sell their
beers. As well as those listed in the text they
handle beers from Géants-Ellezelloise and
brewers from eight other countries, selling to
distributors in 42 States.

Vanberg & DeWulf

52 Pioneer Street, Cooperstown, NY 13326
T 1-800 656 1212 (US only)
E orders@belgianexperts.com
www.belgianexperts.com

In business since 1982 importing Belgian beers
from Boon, Dubuisson, Dupont and Slaghmuylder, plus Castelain from France, for onward
distribution to 30 States at present.

Wetten Imports Inc.

45490 Ruritan Circle, Sterling, VA 20164
T (703) 444 9420   F (703) 703 991 0782
E martin@wettenimporters.com
www.wettenimporters.com

Founded in 1992 and handling the beers of Anker,
Van Honsebrouck and Huyghe, as well as mighty
Samichlaus from Switzerland. Distributes
nationwide.

Index of beer names

Index of beer styles

Pale ale (including Trappist)
De Koninck Amber 45
De Ryck Special 46
Orval 84
Trappist Westvleteren Blond 132

Regional specialties
Bière Darbyste 24
Cervesia 57
Contreras Mars Especial 44
Kerkom Reuss 75

Saison
Biolégère 55
Saison de Pipaix 122
Saison Dupont 59
Vapeur en Folie 123

Scotch ale
Canaster Winterscotch 67

Stout
Buffalo 115
Hofblues 72
Stouterik 100

Strong abbey-style ales (including Trappist)
Abbaye de Val-Dieu Grand Cru 114
Achelse Kluis Trappist Extra Bruin 17
Chimay Grande Réserve 42
Kapittel Abt 118
St. Bernardus Abt 12 106
Trappiste Rochefort 10° 94
Trappist Westvleteren 12° 131

Strong amber ale
Arabier 47
Caracole Ambrée 39
La Moneuse 25

Strong blond ale
Duvel 62
Guldenberg 89

Strong brown ale
Fantôme Black Ghost 64
Gouden Carolus Classic 19
Loterbol Bruin 77
Oerbier 48
Potteloereke 109
Vicaris Generaal 86

Tripel
Allagash Curieux 136
Kerkomse Tripel (Bink Triple) 76
La Rulles Triple 98
Moinette Blonde 58
Reinaert Tripel 85
St. Bernardus Tripel 107
St. Feuillien Triple 99
Westmalle Tripel Trappist 129

Wheat beer
Blanche des Honnelles (Blanche Double) 15
Saison d'Epeautre 26
St. Bernardus Witbier 108

Winter beer
Gouden Carolus Noël 20

Customers browsing the wide selection at the Mi-Orge Mi-Hublon beer warehouse in Arlon

CAMPAIGN
FOR
REAL ALE

Books for Beer lovers

CAMRA Books, the publishing arm of the Campaign for Real Ale, is the leading publisher of books on beer and pubs. Key titles include:

300 Beers To Try Before You Die!

ROGER PROTZ

300 beers from around the world, handpicked by award-winning journalist, author and broadcaster Roger Protz to try before you die! A comprehensive portfolio of top beers from the smallest microbreweries in the United States and family-run British breweries to the world's largest brands, this book is indispensable for both beer novices and aficionados alike.

£14.99   ISBN 978 1 85249 213 7

Good Beer Guide 2009

Editor: ROGER PROTZ

The *Good Beer Guide* is the only guide you will ever need to find the right pint, in the right place, every time. It's the original and best independent guide to around 4,500 pubs and more than 600 breweries throughout the UK. The Guide has previously been named as one of the *Guardian's* books of the year and the *Sun* has rated it in the top 20 books of all time! This annual publication is a comprehensive guide to the best real ale pubs in the UK, researched and written exclusively by CAMRA members and fully updated every year.

£14.99   ISBN 978 1 85249 231 1

CAMRA's London Pub Walks

BOB STEEL

A practical, pocket-sized guide enabling you to explore the English capital while never being far away from a decent pint. The book includes 30 walks around more than 180 pubs serving fine real ale, from the heart of the City and bustling West End to majestic riverside routes and the leafy Wimbledon Common. Each pub is selected for its high quality real ale, its location and its superb architectural heritage. The walks feature more pubs than any other London pub-walk guide.

£8.99   ISBN 978 1 85249 216 8

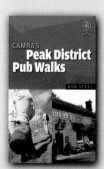

CAMRA's Peak District Pub Walks

BOB STEEL

A practical, pocket-sized travellers' guide to some of the best pubs and best walking in the Peak District, the book features 25 walks, as well as cycle routes and local attractions, helping you see the best of Britain's oldest national park while never straying too far from a decent pint. This book also explores some of the region's fascinating industrial heritage and has useful information about local transport and accommodation. Each route has been selected for its inspiring landscape, historic interest and beer – with the walks taking you on a tour of the best real-ale pubs the area has to offer.

£9.99   ISBN 978 1 85249 246 5

BOOKS

Good Beer Guide West Coast USA

BEN McFARLAND and TOM SANDHAM

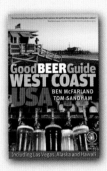

Taking in the whole western seaboard of the USA, as well as Las Vegas, Alaska and Hawaii, this is a lively, comprehensive and entertaining tour that unveils some of the most exhilarating beers, breweries and bars on the planet. It is the definitive, totally independent guide to understanding and discovering the heart of America's thriving craft beer scene, and an essential companion for any beer drinker visiting West Coast America or seeking out American beer in the UK. Written with verve and insight by two respected young beer journalists, *Good Beer Guide West Coast USA* is a must – not just for those who find themselves on the West Coast, but for all discerning beer enthusiasts and barflies everywhere.

£14.99   ISBN 978 1 85249 244 1

Good Beer Guide Prague & The Czech Republic

EVAN RAIL

This fully updated and expanded version of a collectible classic is the first new edition to be published by CAMRA for 10 years! It is the definitive guide for visitors to the Czech Republic and compulsory reading for fans of great beer, featuring more than 100 Czech breweries, 400 different beers and over 100 great places to try them. It includes listings of brewery-hotels and regional attractions for planning complete vacations outside of the capital, sections on historical background, how to get there and what to expect, as well as detailed descriptions of the 12 most common Czech beer styles.

£12.99   ISBN 978 1 85249 233 5

Good Beer Guide Germany

STEVE THOMAS

The first ever comprehensive region-by-region guide to Germany's brewers, beer and outlets. Includes more than 1,200 breweries, 1,000 brewery taps and bars and more than 7,200 different beers. Complete with useful travel information on how to get there, informative essays on German beer and brewing plus beer festival listings.

£16.99   ISBN 978 1 85249 219 9

Good Beer Guide Belgium

TIM WEBB

Now in its 5th edition and in full colour, this book has developed a cult following among committed beer lovers and beer tourists. It is the definitive, totally independent guide to understanding and finding the best of Belgian beer and an essential companion for any beer drinker visiting Belgium or seeking out Belgian beer in Britain. Includes details of the 120 breweries and over 800 beers in regular production, as well as 500 of the best hand-picked cafes in Belgium.

£12.99   ISBN 978 1 85249 210 6

Beer Lover's Guide to Cricket
ROGER PROTZ

There are many books about cricket and many on beer, but this is the first book to bring the two subjects together. Leading beer writer and cricket enthusiast Roger Protz has visited the major grounds of all the First Class counties and gives in-depth profiles of them – their history, museums, and memorabilia, plus listings of the best real ale pubs to visit within easy reach of each ground and details of the cask ales available. This fully illustrated book also features individual sections on the birth of the modern game of cricket and the history of each featured ground, making it an essential purchase for any cricket fan.

£16.99   ISBN 978 1 85249 227 4

Beer, Bed & Breakfast
SUSAN NOWAK and JILL ADAM

A unique and comprehensive guide to more than 500 of the UK's real ale pubs that also offer great accommodation, from tiny inns with a couple of rooms upstairs to luxury gastro-pubs with country-house style bedrooms. All entries include contact details, type and extent of accommodation, beers served, meal types and times, and an easy-to-understand price guide to help plan your budget. This year, why not stay somewhere with a comfortable bed, a decent breakfast and a well-kept pint of beer, providing a home from home wherever you are in the country.

£14.99   ISBN 978 1 85249 230 4

The Book of Beer Knowledge
JEFF EVANS

A unique collection of entertaining trivia and essential wisdom, this is the perfect gift for beer lovers everywhere. Fully revised and updated, it includes more than 200 entries covering everything from fictional 'celebrity landlords' of soap pubs to the harsh facts detailing the world's biggest brewers; from bizarre beer names to the serious subject of fermentation.

£9.99   ISBN 978 1 85249 198 7

A Beer a Day
JEFF EVANS

Written by leading beer writer Jeff Evans, *A Beer A Day* is a beer lover's almanac, crammed with beers from around the world to enjoy on every day and in every season, and celebrating beer's connections with history, sport, music, film and television. Why is 18 April a good day to seek out a bottle of Anchor's Liberty Ale? Which Fuller's beer best marks the date that the Grand National was first run? When would Brakspear's Triple go down a treat? Whether it is Christmas Eve, Midsummer's Day, Bonfire Night or just a wet Wednesday in the middle of October, *A Beer A Day* has just the beer for you to savour and enjoy.

£16.99   ISBN 978 1 85249 235 9

An Appetite For Ale

FIONA BECKETT and WILL BECKETT

A beer and food revolution is underway in Britain and award-winning food writer Fiona Beckett and her publican son, Will, have joined forces to write the first cookbook to explore this exciting new food phenomenon that celebrates beer as a culinary tour-de-force. This collection of more than 100 simple and approachable recipes has been specially created to show the versatility and fantastic flavours that ale can offer. With sections on Soups, spreads & snacks; Pasta, antipasti & risotto; Seafood; Meat feasts; Sweet treats and more, it provides countless ideas for using beer from around the world. With an open mind, a bottle opener and a well-stocked larder, this exciting book will allow you to enjoy real food, real ale and real flavour.

£19.99   ISBN 978 1 85249 234 2

Fuzzy Logic

TOM WAINE

A completely dispensable collection of intriguing nonsense devised or overheard in the pub, compiled and created by regular pub goer Tom Waine. Whether you experience a light-bulb moment while downing a swift half or think you have discovered the meaning of life while imbibing your favourite session beer, this book is packed full of smart ideas, fully-formed theories, unanswered questions – and sheer rubbish. Fuzzy Logic could well leave you entertained, amused and educated for longer than it takes to down a pint.

£9.99   ISBN 978 1 85249 232 8

London Heritage Pubs – An inside story

GEOFF BRANDWOOD and JANE JEPHCOTE

London Heritage Pubs – An inside story is the definitive guidebook to London's most unspoilt pubs. Ranging from gloriously rich Victorian extravaganzas to unspoilt community street-corner locals, the pubs not only have interiors of genuine heritage value, they also have fascinating stories to tell. This book is a must for anyone interested in visiting and learning about London's magnificent pubs.

£14.99   ISBN 978 1 85249 247 2

BOOKS

Order these and other CAMRA books online at
www.camra.org.uk/books,
ask at your local bookstore, or contact:
CAMRA, 230 Hatfield Road, St Albans, AL1 4LW.
Telephone 01727 867201

It takes all sorts to Campaign for Real Ale

CAMRA, the Campaign for Real Ale, is an independent not-for-profit, volunteer-led consumer group. We actively campaign for full pints and more flexible licensing hours, as well as protecting the 'local' pub and lobbying government to champion pub-goers' rights.

CAMRA has 90,000 members from all ages and backgrounds, brought together by a common belief in the issues that CAMRA deals with and their love of good quality British beer. For just £20 a year, that's less than a pint a month, you can join CAMRA and enjoy the following benefits:

A monthly colour newspaper informing you about beer and pub news and detailing events and beer festivals around the country.

A monthly colour newspaper informing you about beer and pub news

Free or reduced entry to over 140 national, regional and local beer festivals.

Money off many of our publications including the *Good Beer Guide* and the *Good Bottled Beer Guide*.

Access to a members-only section of our national website, **www.camra.org.uk** which gives up-to-the-minute news stories and includes a special offer section with regular features saving money on beer and trips away.

The opportunity to campaign to save pubs under threat of closure, for pubs to be open when people want to drink and a reduction in beer duty that will help Britain's brewing industry survive.

Log onto **www.camra.org.uk** for up-to-date CAMRA membership prices and information

CAMPAIGN
FOR
REAL ALE

Do you feel passionately about your pint? Then why not join CAMRA

Just fill in the application form (or a photocopy of it) and the Direct Debit form on the next page to receive three months' membership FREE!*

If you wish to join but do not want to pay by Direct Debit, fill in the application form below and send a cheque, payable to CAMRA to: CAMRA, 230 Hatfield Road, St Albans, Hertfordshire, AL1 4LW. Please note that non Direct Debit payments will incur a £2 surcharge. Figures are given below.

Current rate	Direct Debit	Non DD
☐ Single Membership (UK & EU)	£20	£22
☐ Concessionary Membership (under 26 or 60 and over)	£11	£13
☐ Joint membership	£25	£27
☐ Concessionary Joint membership	£14	£16

Life membership information is available on request.

Title _____ Surname _____ Forename(s) _____

Address _____

_____ Post Code _____

Date of Birth _____ E-mail address _____

Signature _____

Partner's details if required

Title _____ Surname _____ Forename(s) _____

Date of Birth _____ E-mail address _____

CAMRA will occasionally send you e-mails related to your membership. We will also allow your local branch access to your e-mail if you would like to opt-out of contact from your local branch please tick here ☐ (at no point will your details be released to a third party)

Find out more about CAMRA at **www.camra.org.uk**

*Three months free is only available the first time a member pays by DD.

The Direct Debit Guarantee

This Guarantee should be detached and retained by the payer.

DIRECT Debit

- This Guarantee is offered by all Banks and Building Societies that take part in the Direct Debit Scheme. The efficiency and security of the Scheme is monitored and protected by your own Bank or Building Society.

- If the amounts to be paid or the payment dates change CAMRA will notify you 10 working days in advance of your account being debited or as otherwise agreed.

- If an error is made by CAMRA or your Bank or Building Society, you are guaranteed a full and immediate refund from your branch of the amount paid.

- You can cancel a Direct Debit at any time by writing to your Bank or Building Society. Please also send a copy of your letter to us.

✂ ------------------------------------- detached and retained this section

---

CAMPAIGN FOR REAL ALE

Instruction to your Bank or Building Society to pay by Direct Debit

DIRECT Debit

Please fill in the form and send to: Campaign for Real Ale Ltd. 230 Hatfield Road, St. Albans, Herts. AL1 4LW

Name and full postal address of your Bank or Building Society

To The Manager   Bank or Building Society

Address

Postcode

Name (s) of Account Holder (s)

Bank or Building Society account number

Branch Sort Code

Reference Number

Banks and Building Societies may not accept Direct Debit Instructions for some types of account

Originator's Identification Number

| 9 | 2 | 6 | 1 | 2 | 9 |

FOR CAMRA OFFICIAL USE ONLY
This is not part of the instruction to your Bank or Building Society

Membership Number

Name

Postcode

Instruction to your Bank or Building Society
Please pay CAMRA Direct Debits from the account detailed on this Instruction subject to the safeguards assured by the Direct Debit Guarantee. I understand that this instruction may remain with CAMRA and, if so, will be passed electronically to my Bank/Building Society

Signature(s)

Date